M000094651

LOVE YOURSELF LIGHTER

Michelle,

I can't wait
to see what you
create with your
life.

xo,

Suyin Nichols ♡

LOVE YOURSELF LIGHTER

How to End Your Weight Struggle by Changing the Way You Think

SUYIN NICHOLS

Love Yourself Lighter

Copyright © 2014 by Suyin Nichols

This book was written for informational and educational purposes only and is not intended in any way to be a substitute for medical and/or psychological advice, diagnosis, treatment, or therapy from a fully qualified professional. No action should be taken solely on the contents of this book. You as the reader must be responsible for consulting with your own physician or a qualified health professional on any matters regarding your health and wellbeing. The author and publisher are not responsible or liable for any actions or consequential results made by a reader based on the contents of this book and shall not be liable for any damages or costs of any type arising out of, or in any way connected with, a reader's use of this book's contents.

First Edition
Published by Word Love Publishing

ISBN-10: 0-692-32598-0
ISBN-13: 978-0-692-32598-8

Edited with love by Jane Zunkel
Cover and Interior Design by Nu-Image Design

Printed in the United States of America

To Mom.

*For always supporting me in marching to
the beat of my own drum.*

ACKNOWLEDGEMENTS

The book you are holding in your hand began with a thought and is now a reality thanks to the love and support from several wonderful people:

My mother, May Nichols, who celebrated with me each time I completed a chapter and who encouraged me every step of the way.

My coach colleague, Deb Butler, to whom I owe a huge debt of gratitude for being my writing accountability coach. I believe with all of my heart that the outcome of this book would not have been the same without her.

My friend and classmate, Jane Zunkel, who waited ever so patiently for me to finish writing and then generously offered to do the editing for me. Her expert eyes were the first to read my book in its entirety, and the feedback she gave me was priceless.

The members of the best cheering section I could ever ask for are Ally Cox, Gaynor Levisky, Joann MacFarlane, Laura Rosenberg, Lesli Leong, Lisa Hayes, and Mary Ellen Hills. They believed in me and saw me through every moment of self-doubt and procrastination. Their love and enthusiasm kept me motivated to keep going so that I could share this important work with those who need it.

Lastly, my friend and coach mentor, Brooke Castillo, who has never once let me forget my greatness and who has been the most influential friend I have ever had. Without her, I would not be the person I am today. I love her for all that she is and for all that she has inspired me to be.

TABLE OF
CONTENTS

Acknowledgements ix
Introduction 1
My Journey..13

SECTION ONE • Create a Foundation for Change.....................21

Chapter 1 • Recognize Your Wake-up Call....................................22
Chapter 2 • Welcome Vulnerability..24
Chapter 3 • Tell Yourself the Truth 27
Chapter 4 • Live What You Want, Not What You Learned 29
Chapter 5 • Identify the Stories You Tell Yourself........................32
Chapter 6 • Be Willing to Be Wrong...35
Chapter 7 • Ditch Victim Mentality and Take Responsibility......38

Power Thoughts for Section One..41
Inner Wisdom Access Questions for Section One 42
Self-Love Practices for Week One 44

SECTION TWO • Set Yourself Up for Success............................45

Chapter 8 • Let Go of the Past 46
Chapter 9 • Don't Be in a Hurry 48
Chapter 10 • Your Journey Will Be Messy Sometimes 51
Chapter 11 • Be Gentle with Yourself...53
Chapter 12 • Measuring Your Progress Beyond the Scale 55
Chapter 13 • Motivate Yourself with a Positive Why..................59
Chapter 14 • Set Your Intention Each Day....................................62

Power Thoughts for Section Two..64
Inner Wisdom Access Questions for Section Two 65
Self-Love Practices for Week Two 66

SECTION THREE • Your Beliefs, Your Brain, and You 67

Chapter 15 • The Power of Your Beliefs 68
Chapter 16 • Your Beliefs and Your Brain 71
Chapter 17 • The Why Behind Your Weight 73
Chapter 18 • How Your Thoughts Create Your Reality 89
Chapter 19 • Feeling Your Feelings 97
Chapter 20 • You Are a Powerful Creator 102
Chapter 21 • Step Into the Energy of Who You Want to Be 105

Power Thoughts for Section Three 110
Inner Wisdom Access Questions for Section Three 111
Self-Love Practices for Week Three 113

SECTION FOUR • Renew Your Relationship
with Yourself and Your Body 115

Chapter 22 • Change How You Talk to Yourself 116
Chapter 23 • Be Your Own Best Friend 119
Chapter 24 • It's Okay to Like Yourself 121
Chapter 25 • Unwind Media-Driven Perfectionism 125
Chapter 26 • Learn to Love the Body You Live in 128
Chapter 27 • Focus on Your Wellbeing Instead of Your Weight 131

Power Thoughts for Section Four 135
Inner Wisdom Access Questions for Section Four 136
Self-Love Practices for Week Four 138

SECTION FIVE • Reinvent Your Relationship with Food 139

Chapter 28 • Stop Dieting 140
Chapter 29 • End Emotional Eating 143
Chapter 30 • Take the Charge Off of Food...............................147
Chapter 31 • Food is Meant to Be Enjoyed 150
Chapter 32 • Waste It or Wear It..153
Chapter 33 • Think Before You Eat 157
Chapter 34 • Peaceful Eating at Parties and Holidays 160

Power Thoughts for Section Five...164
Inner Wisdom Access Questions for Section Five 165
Self-Love Practices for Week Five 167

SECTION SIX • Let Your Body Lead 169

Chapter 35 • Get Really Good at Body Listening 170
Chapter 36 • Honor Your Hunger and Fullness Cues.................173
Chapter 37 • Nourish Your Body Intuitively.............................178
Chapter 38 • Pay Attention to How Certain Foods Feel in Your Body 180
Chapter 39 • When Comfort Food Becomes Discomfort Food 184
Chapter 40 • See Your Stomach as Sacred Space 186
Chapter 41 • Remind Yourself, "I Don't Do That Anymore".......................188

Power Thoughts for Section Six...191
Inner Wisdom Access Questions for Section Six.........................192
Self-Love Practices for Week Six 194

SECTION SEVEN • Self-Care is Self-Love in Action 197

Chapter 42 • Make Your Self-Care a Priority 198
Chapter 43 • Self-Care as a Daily Practice 201
Chapter 44 • Dress Your Body with Love 211
Chapter 45 • Eliminate Unnecessary Stress Triggers 215
Chapter 46 • Build a Supportive Tribe 222

Power Thoughts for Section Seven 227
Inner Wisdom Access Questions for Section Seven 228
Self-Love Practices for Week Seven 230

SECTION EIGHT • Live Like You Love Yourself 233

Chapter 47 • Love Your Life Now, Not Later 234
Chapter 48 • Happiness is a Habit 239
Chapter 49 • Use Your Life to Inspire Others 242
Chapter 50 • You Are Meant for Great Things 244

Power Thoughts for Section Eight 247
Inner Wisdom Access Questions for Section Eight 248
Self-Love Practices for Week Eight 249

INTRODUCTION

The Diet Mentality Mind is a prison of our own exquisite construction. Every food rule we have adds another brick to its walls; every insult we hurl at ourselves becomes another bar that blocks the imaginary doorway that leads to the life we think we could be living if it wasn't for our weight.

What is Diet Mentality exactly? It's that ever-present voice in your head that tells you that you are not good enough the way you are and if you could just get your body to conform to societal standards of thinness, you would be deemed worthy. This way of thinking causes you to hyper-focus on food, certain parts of your body, your size, your weight, and various numbers in the forms of calories, carbs, the scale, the size tag in your clothing, your BMI, etc. Managing your weight becomes a full-time job and leaves little room for happiness and joy, because your life is forever on hold until you drop those unwanted pounds. You may sporadically experience some weight loss after subjecting yourself to strict dieting or a particularly grueling exercise regime, but those results last only as long as your willingness to keep it up and when you eventually gain the weight back, the cycle of self-loathing begins again.

The signs of having a Diet Mentality Mind are these:

THE SCALE

- You keep a Magic Number (scale weight) in your head and you compare yourself to this number on a regular basis. If you are above this number even by a pound, in your mind you have fallen short.
- The number on the scale dictates your day.
- You obsessively weigh yourself or you avoid the scale like the plague, preferring not to know.
- You remove all clothing and jewelry before getting on the scale
- There are two different weights: Pre-poo and post-poo.
- You weigh in at the doctor's office and quickly calculate how much of that is your clothes and meals.
- You'd never dream of weighing yourself at the end of the day or anytime after a meal.
- You allow the number to determine your worth as a human being.

FOOD

- You know the calorie counts of most foods and beverages.
- You make yourself eat tasteless food when you are dieting.
- You engage in "last chance eating" right before beginning a diet.

- You deprive yourself, only to binge later.
- You often don't even taste the food you're eating.
- Eating healthy is all or nothing.
- You give food power over you.

CLOTHES

- You have various sizes in your closet ranging from "thin" clothes to "fat" clothes.
- You wear clothes that are too tight because you refuse to go up a size.
- Bathing suit shopping is your worst nightmare.
- You judge yourself based on the number on the size tag in your clothes.
- You have a magical clothing size number in your head and you think that if you could only wear that size, life would be perfect.
- You treat yourself to nice clothes only if you are "thin."
- You are generally uninspired by your wardrobe unless you are "thin."

SOCIAL/RELATIONSHIPS

- You're constantly comparing yourself to other people.
- You dread going to parties because you're afraid you'll be too tempted by the food. Or, you love going to parties because you can spend the entire evening with the buffet table.
- It's hard for you to be happy for a friend's weight loss success.

- Your thoughts about your weight keep you from dating or being intimate with the partner you already have.
- You scan the room to see where you fall between the heaviest and the thinnest person in the room.
- You don't set boundaries with other people because you're afraid they won't like you if you did.

SELF

- You live in a fun-free zone created by your mind.
- You have low self-esteem.
- You put your life on hold until you meet the conditions you've set for yourself regarding your weight.
- You don't go for the promotion or change careers to something you'd actually love because of your thoughts about your weight.
- Your preoccupation with your weight has been a substitute for living your life.

That is quite a list! Just reading it is exhausting enough, but if you are living this way, it's a sobering look at where a huge chunk of your energy is going. To acknowledge this as a way of life seems absurd at first, but this may be what you've come to know as "normal." These behaviors have been cultivated over time and are reinforced culturally and by several industries that profit from any kind of fear you may have about not being good enough. When you tie your self-worth to your weight, you buy into the lie that you're not good enough and remain in the prison you've built for yourself.

If you're like millions of other people who have been struggling with their weight, my guess is that up until now, you've believed that you had to be mean to yourself to inspire change. You have been using tools such as self-hatred, shame, and guilt to motivate yourself. On occasion, you might have succeeded in torturing yourself slim but then lived in terror trying to maintain it. You thought that thinness guaranteed happiness, and you have been disappointed that you were still miserable in a thinner body.

You've lost and gained the same pounds countless times, making your body your enemy along the way. Over and over you have blamed your body for your unhappiness. You vacillate between abusing it and ignoring it altogether. You haven't cared for your body in a consistent way because let's face it: Why would you care for something you hate or don't acknowledge?

If the methods you have been using to create the freedom you seek have never led you to peace around food and feeling good in your body, how much more evidence do you need to collect before accepting that hating your way to health doesn't work?

What if I told you there was another way? What if the way out of diet mentality prison was not through changing your body, but through *changing your mind?*

Like everyone else, you have believed that food and/or your body was the problem. They're not. The problem is the way you think. Your mind is like a very powerful computer. The things you focus on are what your mind seeks out to create for you. It has been working all this time; it's just that it has been programmed incorrectly. Right now you have old software running the show and the program is set on "weight struggle."

This is why willpower doesn't work. If you struggle with your weight, you have a belief system that is causing you to hold on to extra weight or gain it back whenever you lose it. Beliefs like to be proven true at all times. Let's say your belief is, "I'll never lose this weight," but then you go on a diet or start exercising and you start to lose weight. Your new result does not match your original belief, so there is tension (it's called cognitive dissonance, more on this later). To alleviate the tension, you either have to change the belief to match your new result (a slimmer body), or you have to gain the weight back. Since you didn't know that your beliefs are causing you to carry extra weight in the first place, you've had no clue that you needed to change the belief to relieve the tension. The only thing available to you (up until now) was to sabotage your new healthy habits and gain the weight back so that the belief of "I'll never lose this weight" can be proven true. Unfortunately, you've been taught to label your attempt at relieving the tension as "lack of willpower." It's not your fault that you have sabotaged yourself; it's just your mind doing its job as efficiently as possible.

So, see? You are not weak, you are not hopeless, and you do not lack willpower. You are none of the mean things you've been telling yourself. At some point you subconsciously programmed your mind to hold on to extra weight. The good news here is that you can reprogram it! What you'll want to do is upgrade the software. When you are operating on a new program in your mind, you will create new results in your life.

Since your mind is always working, why not program it to your advantage? By following the process outlined in this book, you will become aware of your mind's current programming; plus you'll learn how to unwind detrimental thought patterns and replace them with brand new ones that support a healthy body and a happy mind. Get ready to swap body hate for body love, create a harmonious relationship with food, and learn to like yourself again.

Even if you've been down on yourself for years, know that feeling good about yourself is an option available to you. Cultivating a Wellbeing Mind will take some practice, and here is what you can look forward to when you do:

A WELLBEING MIND

- You nourish your body with delicious, satisfying food.
- You naturally honor your hunger and fullness cues.
- Everything in your closet fits your body now and is a delight to wear.
- You focus on the people and the conversations at parties or when out with friends. Food is secondary. Food can certainly add to the experience, but it is not the focus of it.
- You can appreciate people as they are while appreciating yourself at the same time.
- Your conversations no longer focus on weight and dieting.
- You have the desire and the energy to pursue hobbies and interests that enrich you (art, language, writing, dancing, sports, travel, etc.).
- You are intimate with and loving to yourself, which ripples out into your friendships and other relationships.

- You like who you are and you enjoy your own company.
- You measure the greatness of your life, not in the number of pounds lost but in the number of unforgettable experiences you create for yourself.

On this journey, you will be gathering lots of new information and will learn many powerful lessons along the way. Here are some important reminders before you get started:

1. THIS IS NOT A DIET! You do not need to prepare for the impending doom of deprivation with what I call *front-loading* or *last chance eating* because there is no deprivation in the *Love Yourself Lighter* method. A healthy lifestyle does not have to be restrictive, so the habit of harming your body right before you attempt to heal it can end today.

2. Your body is precious, and it wants to be healthy. It is a miraculous vessel equipped with survival mechanisms designed to keep you alive and functioning. Cultivate a loving partnership with your body and learn to work with it instead of against it. Remind yourself often that you and your body are on the same side.

3. Unlike other books out there that focus solely on taking immediate action (eat less, move more), this book is very different. My guess is that you already know how to take action, but you have yet to address the emotional component of the weight struggle that has been keeping you stuck. Here you will be guided through a process to help you clear out any

mental blocks you may have *before* you start taking self-care actions. I invite you to trust the process and not skip the most important part—exploring your mind and understanding how the way you think is affecting the quality of your life.

4. Think of exploring your mind like you are discovering a new world. Every belief you unearth, every new thing you learn about yourself is fascinating and exciting. Like any good explorer, you will want to document your findings. You'll also want a place to expand upon some of the ideas you'll be learning about in this book. Treat yourself to a journal and a pen that you'll love to use and allow them to be your trusted companions during this life-changing adventure.

5. Don't just read this book—DO this book. At the end of each section, you will find a set of tools that correspond with the chapters in that section. Use these tools to help you rewire your mindset toward success:

Power Thoughts: The words you say in your mind or speak out loud are very powerful in creating your outcomes. The Power Thoughts in each section have been carefully crafted to help you embody the lessons within the chapters you read. Start off by picking **one** Power Thought from the list of ten that you think you would benefit from practicing the most (you will learn to how modify a thought to make it more believable to you in Chapter 18). Write it out on a sticky-note or a 3x5 card and put it in a place where you can see it often (your bathroom mirror, on your computer, etc.), or you can take a picture of it with your phone and make it the home screen so that you'll see it every time you use it. Practice repeating your Power Thought throughout the day until it feels solid. Once it does, you can pick another one from the list and repeat the process. Ultimately, you want to fill your mind with a collection of positive thoughts that will help you create the results you want.

Inner Wisdom Access Questions: All of the answers you will ever need to end your weight struggle already reside within you. You just need some really good questions to draw them out! The Inner Wisdom Access Questions have been specifically designed to help you explore your mind and understand your thinking better, or they will help you engage your mind in the process of creating the outcomes you desire. You may surprise yourself with some of the answers that surface. Please don't judge yourself for any truths you reveal. Be as compassionate with yourself as you would with your best friend who was sharing her innermost thoughts with you.

Weekly Self-Love Practices: Many of you may want to use this book as a self-coaching program, so I have included Self-Love Practices to follow each week to go with the material in each section. There are eight sections in the book, so the self-coaching program will last eight weeks. Each week you will be invited to practice at least one thought from the Power Thoughts list; answer the Inner Wisdom Access Questions in your journal; and practice one or two self-coaching tools for the following seven days.

In Week One you are invited to begin keeping a food journal, and I recommend using this valuable tool for the *full eight weeks*. This is not a diet journal; this is an *awareness* tool. Think of it like you are collecting data for a science experiment. There's no emotional charge when it's research, right? You are the fascinating subject you are learning about, and your food journal is where you will log your findings. Start with a simple food journal where each day you log the time and what you ate or drank (Remember, no judgment—it's just data). Later in the book, you will be invited to tweak your food journal a bit to practice some of the awareness skills you will be learning. You will need your food journal to connect with yourself and your body throughout the self-coaching program, so please don't skip this step!

Though this book is designed to help you end the weight struggle, this journey is so much bigger than that. It's not about fast-forwarding to your goal weight—it's about changing the mindset that has caused you to struggle with your weight in the first place. When you eliminate the cause (faulty thinking), you eliminate the symptom (excess weight). With this method other things get eliminated, too, such as obsessive thoughts about food; body hatred; and low self-esteem. The lightness you will feel will go way beyond mere scale weight because you will finally be free of the soul-sucking mental burden of the Diet Mentality Mind.

Behind the negative stories you keep telling about yourself, you are already the person you want to be. You don't have to keep chasing what you already have. Through this book, I will help you see yourself more clearly than you ever have before, and over time, you will begin to reveal the unmistakably wonderful You you've been hiding underneath the weight struggle. It's okay if you're scared. I'm inviting you to step out of your comfort zone and try a bunch of new things. Allow yourself to trust the process, commit to the practices within the book, and be willing to *Love Yourself Lighter*.

My Journey

When I was growing up, I never thought about my weight. I was too busy playing and enjoying everything I could create with my imagination. My two older brothers died when I was a baby, leaving me an only child, so I learned how to enjoy my own company at an early age. I would sing and dance to Disney soundtracks on my record player, climb trees, ride my bike to the park, get lost in the world of my Barbie dolls, and comb through stacks of picture books, allowing my mind to take flight. Oh, and I watched a ton of cartoons. Like many children, the TV was my baby sitter. I didn't mind that I was alone most of the time. I liked myself and knew how to have fun.

In the early part of my childhood, I split my time between my mom's house and my grandmother's house. My mom worked the midnight shift at the Postal Service and slept during the day, so I stayed with Gran on the weekdays and spent the weekends with Mom. My experience of food was very different in the two houses. At Gran's, the kitchen was filled with the aroma of home-cooked meals made in an iron skillet, using bacon grease from a coffee can next to the stove. I ate a variety of foods including oxtail stew, squid with vegetables, and my all-time favorite, bacon, eggs & rice with soy sauce. At Mom's house, I remember fast food, Swanson's TV dinners, Hostess treats wrapped in foil, and sugary cereals in brightly-colored boxes with a prize inside. On Sundays, Mom and I would ride our bikes to Denny's coffee shop and I'd have the same thing every time—Pigs in a Blanket (sausages rolled up inside of pancakes) drowning in butter and syrup. Back then I didn't think much about food. It was merely a break to fuel up for the hours of creative play I couldn't wait to get back to.

When I was eight years old, my two worlds merged. Mom sold her house, Gran sold her house, and the three of us moved into a new, bigger house together. Mom switched to a day job and I saw her more often. I also saw her dieting. She was always on Weight Watchers or following some other plan detailed out on a smelly piece of ditto paper. I remember Tupperware containers filled with tuna and lettuce and tubs of cottage cheese in the fridge. Gran kept right on with her home cooking to feed herself and me.

I never paid attention to my mom's dieting, and for the next few years, I didn't place any focus on my own body either. I just had fun. I did gymnastics, took dance classes (Jazz & Tap—oh, the sequins!), played tennis, and really enjoyed ice-skating. I was quite good at it, so Mom stopped signing me up for group classes and hired a coach for private lessons. The ice rink is where I first learned how to judge my body.

I was eleven years old when Mom took me on a vacation to Mexico. Somehow I accidentally drank the water, and I spent three solid days in our hotel room recuperating from Montezuma's Revenge. All I could eat was boiled eggs and bananas. I don't know how much weight I lost, but I remember feeling very weak when I returned to the ice rink. My blades barely touched the ice before my peers and other coaches skated up to me to congratulate me on how thin I looked. I got so much attention and praise that I'm certain that's the exact moment that the belief, "Being thin is a good thing" was implanted in my mind.

By the next year, I had switched skating coaches and started skating at a different rink. I also started growing, and my body began filling out. My new coach had a weigh-in policy; every week we had to step on the scale in front of our peers. She decided I was "too fat" and put me on a liquid diet of nasty, powdered shakes made in a blender. I was twelve. I would skate for hours on this restricted calorie diet, and I was always hungry and weak. Though my mom went along with the coach's diet recommendations as part of my "training," occasionally she would sneak me food to give me some energy for skating. My coach caught me eating once and berated me in front of the whole rink. I felt so full of shame. That day I learned that food was bad and that I was bad for eating it. By age fourteen I quit skating. I had learned to hate it and everything associated with it. I had also learned to hate my body. I was taught that my body was wrong, that it was a thing that needed to be controlled. I came away believing that I was not good enough and that the scale dictated my worth.

Starting high school with my weight in the forefront of my mind, I decided to join my mom in trying out a new diet program called Nutri/System. For months I ate shelf-stable food that came in tin cans and foil packets that we purchased at the Nutri/System center. Though I felt like an astronaut eating space food, I did lose weight and stayed pretty steady for most of the school year after transitioning back to regular food bought in a supermarket. By sophomore year, I started driving, and my weight slowly started creeping up since I was no longer walking to and from school. By my junior year, Gran's doctor told her she had to stop driving and instructed my mom to take away her car keys. Gran didn't want to live without her independence, so on Christmas Day that year, she decided that was going to be her last meal and began the process of starving herself to death. Her slow decline took five months. As her weight went down, mine started going up. Looking back, I see that I was subconsciously eating for both of us since I believed that food would have saved her life. She weighed only 60 pounds when she died. Nearly thirty years have passed, and I still cry when I think about it.

At the end of my senior year of high school, I weighed 40 pounds more than when I was dieting my freshman year. My weight fluctuated up and down the same 15-20 pounds for the next two years. My 21st birthday was coming up, and I wanted to look awesome at my birthday party, so I got a job as a receptionist at Nutri/System because employees got a 50% discount on the food. I also got the inside information on the calories, since back then the packages were not labeled with the nutritional information on them. I soon manipulated the calorie counting into borderline anorexia. I subsisted on a ½ cup of cereal with a ½ cup of skim milk for breakfast; I ate my pre-packaged dinner meal for lunch with a side of plain steamed veggies, and I would nibble on some kind of gummy fiber snacks at work in the evenings to stave off my raging hunger. Starvation, coupled with two-hour daily workouts, caused me to drop a lot of weight by my birthday. What I probably lost was a bunch of muscle tissue, but I cared only about what the scale said. I was THIN. *I was thin for three days.* I couldn't maintain the calorie restriction, and my weight started going right back up. I quit working Nutri/System a year later but remained in the full-time job that is the weight struggle for the next 15 years.

Though I never returned to that level of starvation dieting, I continued my quest to change my body. I bought so many books, gym memberships, and DVD's from infomercials. I tried juice fasts, cleanses, and some scary herbal diet pills that were eventually taken off the market due to reported deaths. I sometimes secretly dreamed about going back to Mexico and bringing back bottles of tap water in hopes of recreating the weight loss I experienced when I was eleven. Sick, I know. I kept putting on more weight due to the last chance eating I was doing leading up to each diet, and then the subsequent binging afterwards. I "dieted" my way up the scale to the tune of 50 more pounds on my frame. I was obsessed with food and was constantly fixated on what and when I could eat next. Too many nights I sat on my bedroom floor, crying my eyes out, surrounded by empty packages of chips, cookies, and containers of ice cream. I consumed it all until it was gone. How was it possible that I could I feel so full and feel so desperately empty at the same time? I hated myself, and I was miserable.

With all this abuse I was heaping on my body, by 2005 I had developed a horrible case of gastroesophageal reflux disease (GERD), and my blood pressure was climbing. I was so sick that I finally hit my own personal rock bottom. I told myself that I was too young to feel this bad and made an appointment with my doctor immediately. I began my path to healing that day by following the nutritional guidelines given to me by my doctor. Within two months, I had healed the GERD without the use of drugs. I felt inspired! It was the first time I realized that I could create results by caring for my body, rather than being at war with it.

My quest to heal my body continued. They say that when the student is ready, the teacher appears. I was ready, and the teacher appeared in the form of an amazing weight loss coach who helped me to untangle the emotional ties I had to the extra weight I carried on my body. This was an awesome, life-changing experience. There were days that I cried during this process, too, but this time they were tears of relief because I had finally learned how to feel my feelings instead of eating them. I shed 45 pounds of fat and gained lean muscle mass by eating healthy and being consistent with my workouts. I fell in love with coaching and how transformational it is, and I eventually became a coach myself in 2009.

Learning to manage my mind has been the single most important life skill I have ever learned. This skill was tested when I developed plantar fasciitis and bone spurs in my feet. Because of the excruciating nerve pain, I could no longer exercise as intensely as I had been and over time, I gained back about 20 pounds. At first this felt awful—not the actual weight gain but the awful stories

I was telling myself about it. "How can I be a weight loss coach when I've gained weight?" There were times when I felt like a fraud, but then I reminded myself that I was still using the coaching tools I was teaching; it's just that the amount of exercise I was able to do while injured created a body that happened to weigh more. I stopped telling myself mean stories and asked myself this question instead: "What is perfect about this weight gain?" My answer was this:

> *"Suyin, this weight gain is here to teach you how to love yourself, regardless of what your body weighs. Even though you have been very good at managing your mind, it has come to light that there is still a little part of you that remains attached to the number on the scale. You are WAY too amazing to limit your worth to a three-digit number. You manifested this experience to learn how to truly care for yourself and your body in a way like never before. You will eventually teach what you learn to others who are desperately seeking a way to silence their Diet Mentality Mind and get on with living a life they love."*

Inspired by the answer to my own question, I began to immerse myself in the art of loving self-care. I studied my body and listened to how it wanted to be nourished. I learned to work with my foot injury instead of succumbing to it and figured out how to rebuild my strength in a gentler way. I learned how to care for myself beyond my body by creating healthy boundaries and actively avoiding negativity and drama. Though I have released half of the weight I had regained and still continue in the downward trend, the preoccupation with my weight has been replaced by a strong sense of self and a propensity to seek out what's good in the world around me. I like who I am and finally feel at home in my body. I am now channeling the energy I used to spend focusing on my weight into more creative passions, like writing this book. It is my deepest wish that the sharing of the knowledge I have gathered on my own journey inspires others to believe that they no longer have to live in Diet Mentality prison and as they turn the pages, they collect the keys to set themselves free.

SECTION ONE

CREATE A FOUNDATION
FOR CHANGE

CHAPTER 1

RECOGNIZE YOUR WAKE-UP CALL

Something is off. You see the signs. Or you feel it internally. You begin noticing that you are engaging in behaviors that are causing you to check out of your own life.

Is your wake-up call right in front of you?

Maybe it's the half-eaten jar of Nutella in your pantry that you just bought yesterday or the empty bags of chips, sleeves of cookies, or pints of ice cream that are filling your trash can.

Maybe your wake up call is a health issue. Joint pain? Acid reflux? High blood pressure? Diabetes? Your body might be crying out for your attention, but you are so used to ignoring yourself that you don't even hear it.

Maybe it's in your closet in the pants that you can't zip up, in the space between your blouse buttons that gaps open, or in your swimsuit that never sees the light of day and has yet to touch water.

Maybe your wake-up call can be found in your checkbook, in your credit card statements, or in your bedroom.

Or maybe you've hit rock bottom and you're in an emotional puddle on the floor.

Whatever your particular wake up call is, know that it is a gift from your soul designed to get your attention so that you can discover the amazing person you already are underneath your current suffering. It is an invitation to the journey of profound healing that is available to you at any given moment.

Can you hear it? Can you feel it?

Accepting the invitation will require some effort on your part, but if you think about it, you are already investing effort—it's just that what you are currently creating ultimately doesn't feel good. Know that you could be creating something better with the same amount of energy if you decided to. Acknowledging your wake up call and accepting its invitation is the first step to change.

CHAPTER 2

WELCOME VULNERABILITY

Seeing the leaves turn color in Maine during the second week of October was a special treat for this Californian, but never did I think that a visit to the Mount Desert Oceanarium in Bar Harbor would move me to tears. A stop there was part of our bus tour, and I was expecting something more like an aquarium, but we were led to a quaint building that looked more like a home. Very fitting, because owner David Mills and his wife Audrey absolutely made us feel at home during our visit there. We were invited to sit on benches, folding chairs, and even an antique rocker in this big room with a lobster boat that David used as his stage while he educated our group on Maine's lobster industry.

During his talk, David told us that lobsters must shed their shell several times during their lives. They keep growing, but their shells do not. When they vacate their shells, they are already wearing their new one, but it is more like skin until it hardens. This process takes about six weeks, and during this time, the lobster is soft and vulnerable. I didn't think much of this tidbit of lobster lore until David said something profound. He shared with us that he had experienced some hard times over the past two years and that he questioned teachings about being grateful for his problems, but then he said that the lobster taught him a very important lesson, "When we are soft and vulnerable, that's the best time for growth."

I heard his words and took a sharp breath in. In an instant, I thought of all of my clients who fear leaving their shell of old patterns and beliefs—no matter how confining and miserable it is inside of there—because they don't know who they'd be without it. I realized what a gift David had just given me, and I couldn't wait to pass it on to my clients. I was so moved, that I started to cry on my walk back to the bus. A lovely woman from Tennessee named Brenda touched me on the shoulder and asked me if I was all right. I explained to her what his talk had meant to me and she said, "I know what you mean. I think more happened back there than just a talk about lobsters." I couldn't agree more, Brenda.

Leaving the shell of your old life/self/habits/beliefs might feel a bit scary, but it's tight in there, and there's no more room left to grow. You must choose to step out of your shell and allow yourself to be soft and vulnerable for a short time until you build a new set of beliefs that support the new way of being you desire in your mind. For example, say you have been emotionally eating for a long time and now you want to stop this habit. Begin by deciding that you no longer want to be skilled in the practice of emotional eating and acknowledge that there will be an adjustment period as you learn how to feel your feelings instead of eating them. You are asking yourself to give up the familiar shell of emotional eating for something unknown to you. Until you learn how to construct a new way of thinking that supports the new practice you want to become skilled at, you're out of your shell of familiarity, and this can feel quite vulnerable. Unlike the lobster, when we are out of our shell, there are no real threats other than our own negative thinking, which we have 100% control over. It's okay to be out of your shell, as this is where growth happens. Instead of being afraid of being vulnerable, you can now choose to see it as an amazing opportunity to get yourself to the place you want to be.

There comes a time when the shell is no longer a protector but a way to limit your joyful possibilities. You'll know you've outgrown your shell when you feel stifled, stuck, or stagnant. It feels as if the life you are currently living no longer fits. As with the lobster that abandons its shell as many as twenty times during its lifetime, know that you may need to do the same process several times throughout *your* life. Not every "shedding of the old" will be dramatic, as some shifts may be small but just as effective. Take a good look at your life. Could it be time to shed your shell and allow yourself the space to grow to the next level? If so, no need to be afraid. Soft and vulnerable is actually the goal here, so I say go for it!

"When we are soft and vulnerable,
that's the best time for growth."

~ David Mills

Chapter 3

Tell Yourself The Truth

When you are operating with a Diet Mentality Mind, there is a certain level of denial that you live with every day. You get used to telling yourself lies and have conditioned yourself to believe them. You don't stop to question what you're telling yourself and seem to run on autopilot, as if life is happening to you, instead of you being the one in the driver's seat.

Let's examine the thought, "I deserve a treat." Having a treat on occasion is no big deal, but if you beat yourself up after eating it, is it really a treat? Saying, "I deserve punishment" is more like the truth here, but you don't think to tell yourself that. Imagine what would happen if you started questioning your thoughts and telling yourself the truth about them.

One of the most powerful tools to change something in your life is accepting that you've created it. Let's take the present state of your body, for example. Diet Mentality thinking makes you want to blame the state of your body on other things, but when you do that, you're saying that someone or something else has power over you and that you are helpless. This is another Diet Mentality lie.

It is also a lie that accepting where you are means that you have to stay there. Accepting—and appreciating—the body you are living in doesn't mean that you have to stay that way. In fact, it frees you to change because if you can accept that your current choices create your current body, you will then see that you have the very same power to create something different, something healthier, fitter, and stronger if that's what you want. Accepting is not giving up—Accepting is EMPOWERING!

No matter how much you pretend, no matter how much you choose to live in denial, you cannot fool your body. Whenever you feel confused, upset, or icky, my colleague Sarah Yost says, "There is a lie present." See if you can identify the lie (or hire a coach to help you) and then question it: "Is it true? What is the truth here?" You may have to do some digging to find your answer, but you'll know it's the truth when the buzzing in your body goes away and you feel calm. Telling the truth always feels good to your body.

You can't change what you don't acknowledge. Identify the areas where you feel stuck in your life; then take an honest look at what you're doing to create this outcome. When you admit that you are creating your own stuck-ness, you then enable yourself to change it. Be kind to yourself in this process—the truth does not have to hurt. Being honest with yourself is the powerful, liberating force behind the transformation you'll be making on this journey.

One of the most powerful tools to change something in your life is accepting that you've created it.

CHAPTER 4

LIVE WHAT YOU WANT, NOT WHAT YOU LEARNED

"But that's what my parents did."

Have you ever heard yourself say this to explain why you do what you do? Or maybe you've never said this aloud, but if you look at some of your habits and beliefs, the trail leads right back to one or both of your parents (or whomever were your primary caregivers).

This is all fine and good if those beliefs serve you in a good way. If your parents or caregivers modeled things like how to manage money well, how to respect and enjoy nature, how to value your belongings, or how to stand up for yourself—those are beliefs and habits you probably want to keep. These things add to your life in a positive way and lead you to feel good feelings when you practice them.

On the flip side, say your parents or caregivers modeled behaviors like overeating, overspending, gossiping, or over-giving to the point of being a doormat—and you notice that you are now doing the same—you might want to take a look at how these learned behaviors are serving you. Maybe they initially offer pleasure on a certain level, but once the pleasure wears off, you are left to deal with the consequences that are created by your actions (weight gain, debt, broken friendships, ill health, etc.).

When taking a long, hard look at myself on my own journey, I came to a deep revelation about the behaviors that were modeled for me. My grandmother and my mother were my primary caregivers, and both of them were very good at ignoring their bodies. For instance, at age eighty, Gran had a heart attack while caring for a ninety-eight-year-old blind woman and wouldn't let the ambulance take her to the hospital until she put her charge to bed first. My mom, after just having a major surgery to remove a cancerous tumor, announced that she was "going back to work on Monday," even though she had fluid in her lungs and an infected incision.

I see so clearly now that what I learned was how to ignore my body and how to disconnect from it. It was something that "got in the way" or was a burden. I see why I couldn't love it, why I punished it with strict diets and a barrage of insults. It was a thing that had to be controlled, a thing to take the blame for ruining my life by being overweight.

My mother and grandmother weren't able to teach me something that they never learned how to do themselves. If I wanted to break the cycle and heal my relationship with my body, I had to learn new beliefs and new behaviors on my own. Over time, and with a lot of practice, I have been able to shift into taking really good care of my body. I feel very connected to it now and can easily tune in to its subtle communications. Most importantly, I have learned to love it, and wanting the best for the body I live in has changed the entire game.

If some of the beliefs and behaviors you are currently practicing are causing you the ultimate result of suffering in any way, know that they can be unlearned. Just because your parents believed something doesn't mean that you have to believe the same thing. Just because they did something in a certain way doesn't mean that you have to continue the pattern. Some people subconsciously imitate their parents as if it is somehow honoring them, but there is nothing honorable about suffering. You can honor yourself and your caregivers by living a life you love.

CHAPTER 5

IDENTIFY THE STORIES YOU TELL YOURSELF

We all tell ourselves stories every day. Some stories move us forward on our journey, but often our stories hold us back from reaching our fullest potential. Need an example or three? See if any of these sounds familiar:

"I've never kept the weight off before; I'm not successful at maintaining."

"Everyone in my family is overweight, so I am just destined to be fat."

"Losing weight is too hard; it's not worth it."

By thinking this way, you are programming your mind to create and maintain a state of overweight. By being open to changing the story, you allow yourself the chance to reprogram your mind in order to create different outcomes for yourself. Check out these examples of new stories you could choose to tell yourself instead:

"I have never explored the emotional component of the weight struggle before, so it is possible that I will be able to keep the weight off by using the tools I learn."

"My body belongs to me, not my family, and I get to decide how healthy I want to be."

"Creating a healthy, vibrant body is important to me, and I am worth it."

Being open to changing the story is one thing, but it will require you to allow yourself to be wrong about the old story you've been telling yourself. We want so much to be right, so I say use this trait to your advantage. Tell yourself a new, motivating story and go ahead and be right about that.

I invite you to take out your journal and pen and write out the stories you tell yourself. It may be a little challenging to identify them at first because your stories may feel very familiar to you, but a great way to capture them is to write down how you talk to yourself. What is your inner dialogue? Once you get those words out of your head and onto paper, take a good long look at them. *Are these the stories you want to be telling yourself?* If not, write out some new stories to replace the old ones.

"I'm a failure" becomes *"I am capable"* or *"I am learning just how capable I really am."*

"I'm worthless" becomes *"I am worthy"* or *"I am beginning to know my own worth."*

"I'm a victim" becomes *"I am empowered"* or *"I am in the process of becoming empowered."*

"I am unlovable" becomes *"I am lovable"* or *"I am open to believing that I am lovable."*

Some old beliefs can be swapped out in an instant while some are more stubborn, and they will keep popping up until we make the shift to the new belief. When this happens, remind yourself, "Oh, I used to think that. Now I think this _____." Try this tactic and see if it helps you ease into the new belief.

What other stories are you currently telling yourself? Do they help you create an amazing life? Or do they keep you stuck in the mud? Are the stories you tell yourself about old pain from your past affecting your life today? Whatever the thoughts you're currently entertaining in your mind that are causing you to feel fear or despair, remind yourself that it's just a story, and stories can be changed—or dropped altogether.

You are who you tell yourself you are. If you don't like the results of the story you are currently telling about yourself, make up a new one! Believe what you want to believe about yourself, not what someone else tells you that you should. Changing the quality of your life can be as easy as changing the quality of your stories, so be open to creating some good ones that you believe and practice telling them to yourself often.

You are who you tell yourself you are.

CHAPTER 6

BE WILLING TO BE WRONG

I brought up this idea in the last chapter, but I want to expand on it since it can be a major block for those who are very attached to their beliefs. A belief is a thought that you think over and over again. These are some of the core beliefs that I hear frequently from my clients in my coaching practice:

"I am not good enough."

"I will always struggle with my weight."

"I don't matter."

"I am not lovable."

This list is just the tip of the iceberg, as there are dozens more. What is the core belief you have about yourself that holds you back? Go ahead and think of it now. It's okay, I'll wait.

Got it? Okay, keep it in mind, because we're going to use it in a minute.

The thing about beliefs is that they want to be proven true. This goes for positive beliefs as well as negative beliefs. Whatever your beliefs are, your brain goes to work to seek out or manufacture evidence to support it. Think of one of your limiting beliefs right now and then scan your life for the evidence (Example: If you believe the thought, "I will always struggle with my weight," your evidence might be that you've lost weight many times, but then gained it all back again). Like most people who aren't yet aware of how beliefs work, you might be thinking that you believe this thought because you have evidence to back it up, but the truth is that the belief came *first*, and you have subsequently created the evidence for it with your actions or in the way you interpret things. This is how the brain works, and every outcome you have created in your life is based on what you believe about yourself.

Now, here is where your head might explode a little. You know that limiting belief you have been carrying all this time, the one that you'd like to free yourself from right about now? Well, in order to change it or let it go, you are going to have to allow yourself to be wrong about it.

Yes, you read that right. I am asking you to be wrong. W-R-O-N-G. Wrong.

This is so hard for a lot of us. We hate being wrong about anything and because of this, we stay stuck in our lives. We avoid telling ourselves the truth about the choices we are making that don't necessarily serve us because we don't want to admit to being wrong about those choices. So, to avoid being wrong, we cling to old patterns since that's what feels familiar and safe.

For some, "familiar and safe" is a good enough trade-off for a half-lived life, but is it for you? If it's not, then I invite you to take a really good look at your negative or limiting beliefs and ask yourself, "What if I am wrong about this?" (What if I am wrong about believing that I'll always struggle with my weight? What if it doesn't have to be that way after all?). It might feel a little uneasy at first to question your beliefs this way because if you think about it, you have created a whole life based on those old beliefs. Faulty thinking or not, this is what you currently know. BUT HEAR THIS—your old beliefs are not your identity. You are not your stories, and your past does not have to be your future. Those old beliefs are learned beliefs, and if you were able to learn those, then you are just as capable of learning some new ones.

You get to choose what you want to believe about yourself. You also get to choose the evidence that supports your new beliefs. To make space for your new way of thinking, you will have to allow yourself to be wrong about the old way. And it's okay to be wrong, my friend. In this case, embracing your "wrongness" is your ticket out of emotional pain and a half-lived life.

To make space for your new way of thinking, you will have to allow yourself to be wrong about the old way.

CHAPTER 7

DITCH VICTIM MENTALITY AND TAKE RESPONSIBILITY

A common trait I've noticed in many people who engage in emotional eating is something called Victim Mentality. This is where the person blames other people or external circumstances for what's wrong in their lives. Every victim needs a villain so that they don't have to be responsible for themselves. This behavior is very childlike and disempowering.

People with Victim Mentality think that things are happening *to* them rather than seeing how they are participating in the creation of their own pain. They tell themselves that they don't have a choice when in actuality they are making choices all day long. They choose whom they spend their time with, how they react to things, and what they put into their mouths. They often make the same choices over and over again, even when they have plenty of evidence that what they're doing is not healthy or helpful, but then blame their outcome on someone or something else. This is very stressful because they tell themselves that they have no control. A lot of drama is created where there is none, and the stress continues to mount. In order to suppress the fear/anger/helplessness they cause themselves to feel, they may overeat to quiet the negative feelings. They then feel like they are the victim of the extra weight that accumulates on their body. They will blame their body or their weight for their unhappiness or tell themselves that it's the reason why they can't get the job/relationship/ financial success they say they want.

Do you sometimes indulge in Victim Mentality thinking? Be honest with yourself since you can't create change unless you tell yourself the truth. If you see yourself in the description on the opposite page, don't be too hard on yourself or you'll end up both the victim and the villain at the same time. Actually, that is pretty common. We'll address this more in the chapter about mean self-talk in Section Four.

Okay, so what is the antidote to Victim Mentality? RESPONSIBILITY. And not just plain, old, run-of-the-mill responsibility, but *responsibility without self-blame*. It's taking responsibility for the thoughts you think, the feelings you cause yourself to feel, the actions you take, and the results you create with those actions. You are in charge of you and how you experience your life. When you own that you allow the current state of your body to be what it is, you put yourself in the place of empowered creation. If you have the power to create your current body with the choices you make, then you have the same exact power to create a healthier body if you decide to. Taking responsibility for yourself and your life is a grown-up move. Don't be surprised if you start to respect yourself more for jumping into the driver's seat and taking control of your destiny.

We are all meant to fly! What are you allowing to weigh you down or hold you back? Identify it and then ask yourself, "How much longer am I going to allow this to go on?" We choose our anchors. We also choose our freedom. Which will you be choosing today?

When you own that you allow the current state of your body to be what it is, you put yourself in the place of empowered creation. If you have the power to create your current body with the choices you make, then you have the same exact power to create a healthier body if you decide to.

POWER THOUGHTS
FOR SECTION ONE

I am willing to recognize my wake-up call.

I am open to accepting the invitation my wake-up call is offering me to begin my healing journey.

I welcome the opportunity to grow and change.

Being vulnerable with myself will help me get to know myself much better.

I am willing to be honest with myself.

I can live what I want, not what I've learned.

I improve the quality of my life by improving the quality of the stories I choose to believe about myself.

It's okay to be wrong about some of the things I've been believing because I know better now.

My past does not have to be my future.

I am responsible for myself and how I experience my life.

INNER WISDOM ACCESS QUESTIONS
FOR SECTION ONE

---

1. What are the signs of my wake-up call? (Health problems, late night binges, lack of intimacy with my partner, etc. Write down as many as you notice.)

2. What is the message that my wake-up call wants me to know?

3. The reasons why I know I'm ready for a change are...

4. I am willing to tell myself the truth about... (How many times I go to the drive-thru each week, the stash of candy in my drawer at work, why I'm actually afraid to lose weight, etc.)

5. The things that I learned from my parents or caregivers that really don't serve me are... (Not appreciating my body, serving myself seconds and thirds without checking in to see if I'm still hungry or not, thinking that I'm not good enough, etc.)

6. What are the negative stories I've been telling myself about my weight?

7. What are the positive stories I'd like to tell myself about my weight?

8. What are some of my old beliefs that I'm now willing to be wrong about in order to change them?

9. Some of the victim thoughts I think are... (She hurt my feelings, It's his fault I ate the cookies because he brought them into the house, I don't work out at the gym because I don't feel welcome there, etc.)

10. What are the things I have been allowing that I'm now willing to take responsibility for? (How I let people treat me, the state of my career/relationships/finances, the way I have neglected my body, etc.)

SELF-LOVE PRACTICES
FOR WEEK ONE

• Choose one thought from the list of Power Thoughts to practice this week.

• Begin exploring your mind by answering the Inner Wisdom Access Questions for Section One in your journal.

• Practice taking responsibility for yourself by telling yourself the truth about the choices you've been making. (*Examples: I don't pay attention to my health, I make excuses to avoid exercise, I keep on eating even when I am uncomfortably full, I let people walk all over me, etc.*) Once you have them written down in your journal, you may want to explore further by asking yourself, *"Why might I be doing that?"* It's important to know *why* you're doing something before you can change it.

• Begin keeping a food journal as an awareness tool.* This is not a diet journal, so you don't have to change the way you're eating unless you want to. This practice is to help you start paying attention to yourself. Start by keeping a very simple log each day of what you ate or drank, and the time you consumed it. It helps to write down your entries at the time, rather than trying to remember at the end of the day. No judging yourself, okay? This is data collection only.

If you're using this book as an eight-week self-coaching course, I invite you to commit to keeping a food journal for the full eight weeks to develop the kind of self-connection that leads to lasting success.

SECTION TWO

SET YOURSELF UP FOR SUCCESS

CHAPTER 8

LET GO OF THE PAST

If you're like most people with a history of dieting, you have lost weight before and have gained some or all of it back. You may have even ended up weighing more than before you started. You might feel a certain level of shame that you did not maintain it, especially when you look at old photos or the "thin clothes" you still have in your closet. You may be beating yourself up in subtle and not-so-subtle ways, often comparing yourself to who you thought you once were.

Are you stuck in the past? Are you looking to the past to tell you what you should weigh now? Do you say to yourself, "If only I could weigh what I weighed in high school/college/on my wedding day…"? If so, it's important to know *why* you want to weigh that certain number. In my experience as a coach, one of the main reasons why people fixate on a "magic number" is that they associate it with feeling happy at a particular time in their lives. Since we are taught to believe that happiness is caused by thinness, we've anchored those feelings to the number on the scale back then, and we want to weigh that number again, thinking that it will bring back the happiness we remember.

Well, happiness happens in your mind, not because of external circumstances like your weight, and since none of us can turn back the clock, to spend your precious energy trying to recreate the past makes little sense. You are better off focusing on what you can change from here going forward. You are a completely different person now. You've grown, you've evolved, and you may gravitate to entirely different things than you did before. I invite you to open your mind to creating *brand new* experiences for yourself and design a fresh future from your imagination, not from old, stale blueprints of your past.

No matter your weight history, no matter the abuse you've put your body through, none of that matters now. You do not have to keep beating yourself up anymore. It's time to let go. How can you receive anything new if your hands are still clutching the old? Be courageous and release your grip on your past. You're going to need your hands free to receive all the good coming your way.

CHAPTER 9

DON'T BE IN A HURRY

The diet industry offers us quick fixes, promising very little effort on our part. Rapid results sound so tempting because when you are in emotional pain, you are so desperate to get out of it. You'll do just about anything to make it stop. You think, "The faster the better," so you cut out entire food groups, or go on a crash diet, a liquid fast, or a juice cleanse. You might lose some weight very quickly, but the pounds often return just as quickly and sometimes with a few friends. You have gathered enough evidence by now that "fast" is not getting the job done long-term, so perhaps it's time for a new strategy.

If you think your weight is causing your emotional pain, then it makes sense to think that getting rid of it in a hurry will make the pain go away. Thinking this way is a mistake. Emotional pain is caused by the thoughts in your mind. It's not the extra pounds you carry but what you think about them and what you make it mean about yourself that causes you to feel terrible. The good news here is that you can feel better without ever losing a single pound. You can achieve this by managing your mind. By focusing on changing the way you think, you can start to feel good about yourself, and when you feel good about yourself, you are more likely to take good care of your body, which will produce a different outcome than the one you're producing now.

Knowing and doing are two different things. To make the changes you want to make, you'll need to apply the tools you learn to your life. Yes, this means that effort will be required from you on this journey. Effort gets a bad rap in the dieting world, as if it's something you should avoid. This is such faulty thinking. When you put effort into something—especially into yourself—you value the outcomes you create so much more, and this leads to long-term success.

What you *do* want to avoid as you begin taking action is falling into the all-or-nothing trap that dieting trains us for. Sometimes, doing too much too soon can feel overwhelming, and you'll want to give up before you even get started. A strategy that makes all the difference is slowly adding in healthy new actions *one at a time*. Once the action you're practicing becomes a habit, then add in another one. As you build upon this strategy, soon enough, your new healthier habits naturally crowd out the old ones that don't serve you. Take the time to note in your journal the effects your new actions are having on the state of your body and the quality of your life. It's very motivating to have a journal full of evidence that what you are doing is working.

Watch out for your mind wanting to seek fast results. Notice if you begin to feel impatient. How much time do you allow to pass before you decide if what you are doing is working or not? A day? A week? A month? If you don't see the results you are looking for right away, how quickly do you give up? Here's an excellent question to ponder if you are thinking of giving up on your new health routine because you think results aren't showing up fast enough: Does your body only deserve care if it loses weight for you? Of course not! Your body deserves care every day of the week.

Healthy habits are for the long-term. When you decide to add a new healthy habit into your self-care routine, give it time to produce results. Keep at it, as many changes happen on the inside long before they show on the outside. Don't quit just because you think your progress is slow. Remember that slow progress is STILL progress. Time is going to pass anyway, so if you keep at it, you will end up in an entirely different place than if you quit.

When you put effort into something—especially into yourself—you value the outcomes you create so much more, and this leads to long-term success.

CHAPTER 10

YOUR JOURNEY WILL BE MESSY SOMETIMES

Your journey is never going to be a perfect straight line. Telling yourself that it should be only blocks your ability to succeed. There will likely be obstacles, detours, and more than once, you may need to do a U-turn and head in another direction. This is a process. You will overeat sometimes. You will skip workouts. Your weight will fluctuate. You will try new things, and you might stumble at first. You will cry. You will want to give up. Know that this is normal and totally okay. What will get you into trouble here is insisting on perfection.

Insisting on perfection practically guarantees you'll hold on to the extra weight. Either you're waiting forever on perfect circumstances before you even get started or you stunt your progress with all-or-nothing thinking and quit too soon. The remedy for the perfection infection is allowing failure to be an option. Making friends with failure actually helps you to succeed. Failure isn't bad—it's just feedback for what didn't work. Try a different approach next time. Tweak your strategy a little until you find the right fit for you. Take mainstream ideas and alter them to fit your life. The only "right" way to do something is *the way that works for you*. You will have to figure this out with some good ole' trial and error, but if your strategies are sustainable, you cannot help but succeed.

Being compassionate with yourself as you practice the tools in this book goes a long way. There will always be an adjustment period when you're learning something new. Allow things to be imperfect. Know that you WILL overeat or binge from time to time as you heal your relationship with food and your body. Be easy on yourself when this happens. When you beat yourself up for overeating and tell yourself you've "blown it," you're more likely to eat even more. This reaction is not helpful, and it does not move you forward. Choose to think of it another way, like this: There are roughly 21 meals in a week, so a couple of imperfect ones will not matter in the big picture. The only thing that matters is that you don't let a binge or two make you want to give up on yourself entirely. Just pick up with your self-care wherever you are and keep moving forward. Progress is the goal here, not perfection.

Allow yourself the space to make mistakes and fumble during the learning process. Judging yourself and piling on the "shoulds" only encourages the shame spiral. I know this from experience, and it's a sucky place to be. The next time you are hard on yourself, remind yourself that shame and guilt never created anything beautiful. Be kind to yourself in the process, for you will never reach a happy goal if the road to get there was miserable. Sometimes the inner work required to end the struggle feels messy and gritty at first, but if you stick with it, you will eventually uncover the fine treasure that is *you*.

The only "right" way to do something
is *the way that works for you.*

CHAPTER 11

BE GENTLE WITH YOURSELF

There's a generally accepted belief out there that says in order to create change in your life, you're supposed to use self-inflicted force, pressure, and shame. This might work for a time, but it feels terrible and you don't like yourself much during the process. Then, when this strategy doesn't last, you go right back to square one. This really makes no sense; you want to change to feel better, but making yourself feel worthless in the process never gets you to where you want to go. Have you been trying to shame yourself into changing?

What if you decided to use gentleness to create change instead? Being gentle with yourself means being kind, compassionate, and understanding. It means giving yourself support, encouragement, and love as you take each step towards your goal.

This makes so much sense! When you are struggling with a weight issue, there is often a component of hiding involved (hiding your body, hiding your sexuality, hiding your gifts, hiding from your life). You hide to feel safe. When you berate yourself into change, your natural reaction is to recoil and hide further still. Coaxing yourself out with gentleness creates the feeling of safety. When you feel safe, you allow yourself to emerge from your hiding place and from there you can bloom into who you want to be.

An important side note: *Being gentle with yourself is not the same as coddling yourself.* Coddling is indulgent and leads to unhealthy habits that sound like, "I deserve to eat this" or "I can skip my workout because I've had a rough day." Thoughts like these lead to actions that take you away from your goals. True gentleness will sometimes sound like, "I know I'm going to feel much better if I pass on that second cupcake" or "Taking a walk after work really clears my mind." Thoughts like these lead to actions that result in sustainable change.

Since we all know that harshness doesn't work, I invite you to give gentleness a try. It's a practice, so give yourself ample time to get good at it. Giving yourself a break is not the same thing as giving in or giving up. It's just a kinder way to treat yourself as you move forward on your journey.

CHAPTER 12

MEASURING YOUR PROGRESS
BEYOND THE SCALE

As a weight loss coach, a big part of my job is helping my clients unwind Diet Mentality thoughts that cause them pain. The most challenging thoughts to unwind have been the ones that have to do with the scale. Oh, that number on the scale. Why do we allow it to influence our lives as much as we do?

You could wake up in a happy state, ready to face the world with a smile and then you step on the scale, and your mood changes to foul in an instant. You see the scale shift in the smallest increment in the direction you want it to, and you think you can conquer the world. It's as if the number on the scale tells you if you're good or bad, worthy or unworthy. It seems silly when you read this in black and white, yet the conditioning has been so strong that buying into the lie seems normal and acceptable.

It is such an injustice to yourself to live your life by this lie. Think of how often you allow a number to negate all of your greatness. You might be an excellent parent, a wonderful spouse, an influential member of your community, a star employee, a dynamic entrepreneur, a loving and supportive friend—but none of this matters because you weigh "x". Ridiculous right?

The good news is that this is a learned behavior. The even better news is that it is never the number on the scale that determines your mood or dictates your worth or value as a person—*it's your thoughts about the number that cause you to feel a certain way.* The best of the best news beyond that is that you get to decide what you want to think. Yes, friends, you can choose your thoughts, all day every day. This may be a new concept for some of you, but I promise that it's the truth (more about this in Section Three). Choosing new thoughts is like any other skill: to get good at it, you must practice. What's the alternative? To slog through the realm of "I'm not good enough" for the rest of your days? No, thank you!

The data the scale provides is helpful in only two ways. One, it lets you know if the way you are caring for your body leads to weight loss, weight gain, or weight maintenance, and you can decide to adjust your self-care practices to alter your outcome if you want to. Two, the scale is an extremely brilliant tool for helping you to figure out what you are thinking. I like to refer to scales as Thought Finders. When you stand on it and you begin thinking a slew of negative thoughts about yourself or your body after seeing the number come up in the little window, you can download the thoughts you are thinking by writing them in your journal. Then you can evaluate them and decide if those are thoughts you want to keep or not (more on rewiring your thoughts in Chapter 18).

Consider releasing the learned response of seeing your life through the filter of pounds lost or gained. You and your life are so much more than that! Let's look at other ways you can measure your progress that have nothing to do with the scale, shall we?

1. You notice a massive increase in self-kindness and self-care.
2. You're honing your ability to listen to—*and honor*—your body's cues.
3. You are consistent with implementing and building upon the tools you've been learning on your journey.
4. You're releasing the habit of emotional eating.
5. You see a marked improvement in your fitness level.
6. Your clothes are fitting better or are becoming baggy or loose.
7. You feel healthy and vibrant.
8. You're beginning to compliment yourself.
9. You have an improved outlook on life and an increased sense of wellbeing.
10. You're having lots of FUN.

Success means different things to different people. It's okay to be inspired by someone else, but try to resist the urge to compare yourself to what other people are doing. Teach yourself to focus on what you're doing that's moving you forward. Not only will you feel good about yourself, but you are also more likely to repeat those same behaviors tomorrow. When you build yourself up by celebrating even the smallest successes, the positive effects are cumulative and will keep you motivated while reducing the desire to quit.

Keep reminding yourself that success is measured by so much more than the number on the scale. One of my clients wrote to me and said that her doctor had cut her medication down to a quarter of what she was taking and believed that if she continued on her current health path, she'd be off the medications altogether within three months. She said that this measure of progress was far better than merely scale weight. Another client shared with me that her mother asked her, "What's your target?" (as in the number on the scale) and she replied, "My target is my wellbeing." I can't tell you how much I loved hearing this!

When you engage in the practice of focusing on all that's good in your life, you'll begin to notice that the more you do that, the less you focus on your body, except to care for it better. Stepping on a scale will eventually hold no charge anymore because all it will be to you is numerical data. You will be too busy measuring your progress in fun ways that light you up, like how many times you laughed in a day or how much peace you can relax into. Oh, the possibilities!

Consider releasing the learned response of seeing your life through the filter of pounds lost or gained. You and your life are so much more than that!

CHAPTER 13

MOTIVATE YOURSELF WITH A POSITIVE WHY

How many times have you felt disgusted standing in front of the mirror, calling yourself names and vowing to lose weight? How many times have you actually started the diet on Monday, only to give up shortly after? Why do you think you couldn't stick with it? My guess is that when your motivation to do something is fueled by self-hate, it feels terrible and unappealing to continue long-term.

There is always a reason behind why you do anything. To be successful, the "WHY" behind any meaningful goal has to be one that is born out of love. For instance, you can't hate your way to healthy—the two just don't vibe. It's okay to want to change or improve yourself; just make sure you're doing it because you love yourself too much not to.

If you remember from the story of my journey in the beginning of the book, I mentioned the horrendous case of gastroesophageal reflux disease I created for myself from years of abusing my body with food. My digestion was totally out of whack. Sometimes I couldn't keep food down, and the cruise vacation I had saved up for was totally ruined because I spent most of it curled up in pain in my tiny cabin. *That was my rock bottom moment.* I decided right then and there that I was too young to waste my life feeling this bad and set my mind on healing my body. The actions that followed were not fueled by self-hate as so many diet attempts had been in the past. This time my actions reflected the care I chose to give myself, and over time, I loved myself well.

Your body and your life tell the story about how you treat yourself and what you think you deserve. What story are you telling with the state of your body and the state of your life? Is that the story you *want* to be telling? If it's not and you want to make change for the better, then I invite you to come up with a positive WHY to help fuel your actions. For me, my mind was set on feeling healthy, vibrant, and alive. Thinking this way motivated me to keep moving towards what I wanted. What are the things you want? How do you want to feel? I invite you to take out your journal and make a list of your WHY's and phrase them in a positive way (example: "I want to feel strong and energetic" rather than "I don't want feel like a lazy slob anymore").

As you start to plan your strategy to create what you want, you might want to consider adding in the elements of FUN and PLAY. More often than not, force inspires resistance. If your goal is health, the last thing you want to do is resist the very things that will get you there. Fun and play inspire motivation, so seek out ways you can turn healthy eating and exercise into joys you want to return to again and again. When you make something more fun, you're more likely to do it.

When creating your WHY, I invite you to wish bigger than a surface goal of simply losing weight. Think about the person you want to be, how you want to live your life, and all the joyful experiences ahead of you. Think about how the dream you have for yourself can have a positive impact on other people. WISH BIG and know that anything you dream for yourself is yours when you set your mind to achieving it.

More often than not, force inspires resistance.
If your goal is health, the last thing you want to do
is resist the very things that will get you there.
When you make something more fun,
you're more likely to do it.

CHAPTER 14

SET YOUR INTENTION EACH DAY

Each day you get an opportunity to move yourself closer to who you want to be, or further away. Small actions add up to big changes in either direction. By setting your intention each morning, you are programming your mind to drive your actions for the day. If you wake up on autopilot thinking thoughts such as, "Life sucks" or "I'm such a fat pig," you will have an entirely different kind of day than if you purposely stated to yourself, "My choices matter, so I focus on choosing the best options available to me" or "I choose to wait until my body says it's hungry before I eat again." Remind yourself of the intention you set throughout the day if you need to, especially when you've taken an action you'd rather you hadn't.

I mentioned in a previous chapter that sometimes your journey is messy. If you overeat or skip a workout, you do not need to wait until tomorrow to start over. You can choose your direction in any given moment. Start over right here, right now with the very next choice you make. Refocusing your intention can happen *anytime*—in the next hour, the next minute, the next breath. You certainly don't have to wait until Monday to begin again. Begin where you are and keep moving forward.

Should you ever experience a setback (like an illness or an injury), choose to *pause* rather than use it as an excuse to backslide. Your intention could sound something like, "I intend to be caring and patient with myself while I heal" or "I am listening closely for the message this illness/injury has to tell me." Sometimes a perceived setback isn't a setback at all. Sometimes we need to slow down or change directions, and our bodies use illness or injury to get our attention. Rather than choosing to be upset by it, look to see how this might be happening *for* you instead of *to* you. What you first saw as a setback might prove to be the very gift needed to help you evolve to the next level.

How will you use this day you are given? Will you use it to stay stuck? Will you use it to sink yourself deeper into emotional suffering? Or, will you use it to be nice to yourself, to treat your body with loving care, and build upon your goals and dreams? Your daily intention can be broad ("No matter what, I am going to be kind to myself today") or it can be very specific ("I am riding my bike for 45 minutes this afternoon at 4:00 PM"), and it may change from day to day depending on the goals you choose for yourself. Be sure to set your intentions with love, always aiming for your highest good.

By setting your intention each morning,
you are programming your mind to
drive your actions for the day.

POWER THOUGHTS
FOR SECTION TWO

I'm now focusing on what I can create from here going forward.

My body deserves care every day of the week.

Slow progress is still progress—and that's why I won't give up.

By allowing failure to be an option, I give myself the chance to succeed.

I offer support and encouragement to myself as I try out the new things I'm learning.

I am way too amazing to measure my life in pounds lost or gained.

I get to decide how valuable and worthy I am.

I seek out ways to make my journey fun.

My choices matter, and they make a difference in my outcome.

I program my mind for success by setting an intention every day.

INNER WISDOM ACCESS QUESTIONS
FOR SECTION TWO

1. I leave the past in the past by forgiving myself for...

2. The three actions I am willing to add in slowly to my self-care plan are...

3. When my journey gets messy, the supportive things I will tell myself are...

4. What are some ways I could be gentler with myself?

5. What am I already doing well? (It's okay to give myself some credit!)

6. What's the story my body and my life are telling about me right now?

7. What is the story I want my body and my life to tell about me instead?

8. Besides weight loss, what are some of the things I want for myself and my life?

9. What are the Positive WHY's behind those things I want?

10. What is the intention I'd like to set for my *Love Yourself Lighter* journey?

SELF-LOVE PRACTICES
FOR WEEK TWO

- Continue making simple daily entries in your food journal. Are you starting to notice any patterns? If so, be curious about it. What do you think might be driving those patterns? Log your thoughts in your journal.

- Choose at least one thought from the list of Power Thoughts to practice this week.

- Set yourself up for success by answering the Inner Wisdom Access Questions for Section Two in your journal. The answers you come up with will help you provide support for your mind during your journey.

- Practice setting one intention at the start of each day. You can write it on a sticky note to remind yourself throughout the day if you need to. Repetition of your intention trains your brain to make it happen.

- Practice being gentle and patient with yourself as you learn new concepts and try out new ideas suggested in this book. Self-kindness will encourage you to keep moving forward.

SECTION THREE

YOUR BELIEFS, YOUR BRAIN, AND YOU

CHAPTER 15

THE POWER OF YOUR BELIEFS

Most diet books, weight loss articles in magazines, and fitness infomercials on TV focus only on external actions. Eat less, move more. We've all heard it a thousand times. What they never address is the internal component of the weight struggle: YOUR MIND. What you believe, your mind will create for you. You can eat celery sticks and run on the treadmill for hours, but if you have a belief that you will always struggle with your weight, then you will sabotage yourself so that you will "always struggle with your weight." It's the same thing with telling yourself that you need to lose ten pounds. You are programming your mind to create a body that is always in need of losing ten pounds.

Your mind is like a computer. Whatever you program into it, your mind is going to go to work to make that happen. It is a natural law that your belief and your outcome have to match. You will know which beliefs are strongest by the results in your life. For example, you could believe that you want to be thinner than you are, but if your body does not reflect that, then there is definitely a stronger belief overriding it. That belief could be something like, "I'm so fat" or "I'm afraid of getting my heart broken and if I think I'm overweight, I won't put myself out there." Both of these beliefs will cause you to take the actions required to make sure you carry extra weight on your body. Your mind is efficient at making it happen for you, just the way it was designed to.

Don't you ever wonder why when you make efforts to change your daily habits and you start to see some results, you end up sabotaging yourself? This is caused by cognitive dissonance. Your mind cannot hold two conflicting beliefs at the same time. If you think, "I'll never lose this weight" and then you start to lose weight, your belief and your outcome don't match. This creates a strong feeling of tension. To break the tension, you either have to change your belief to something that matches the new outcome, or you have to gain the weight back to match the original belief. The judgmental Diet Mentality Mind would label the self-sabotage caused by this tension as "going off track," "falling off the wagon," or "lacking will power." I want you to know that this is a totally normal response and that there is nothing wrong with you. You just have some old belief systems that need unwinding, that's all.

Your belief systems want to be proven true, no matter what. You have done a great job all these years proving your beliefs true, hence the results you currently have. It's just that the thoughts you are currently thinking do not bring you peace, nor the results you say you want. To end this cycle, you must locate the underlying beliefs and then create new, positive beliefs to replace them. In this case, some replacement thoughts for "I'll always struggle with my weight" become "I'm in the process of creating the healthiest body I can" or "I am becoming a fit and healthy person." Remember to pick better thoughts that you actually believe; otherwise, your mind will reject them (more on this later in Chapter 18). When you choose to replace your old beliefs with new beliefs and then you set out to prove those new beliefs true, that's when you can create and maintain your natural weight in a peaceful way.

Your mind is like a computer. Whatever you program into it, your mind is going to go to work to make that happen.

CHAPTER 16

YOUR BELIEFS AND YOUR BRAIN

A thought is a sentence in your mind, and a belief is a thought you think over and over again. Who you are and how you live your life is a reflection of what you believe. Every action you take is driven by a thought that you are thinking. Thoughts are things and each one has a physical home in your brain. It's called a neural connection. Every time you think a new thought, a neural connection gets created in your brain. Every time you practice this thought and actually believe it, a myelin sheath wraps around the neural connection and makes it stronger. The more you practice thinking a thought, the faster you can recall it until it becomes automatic. The brain is efficient and doesn't keep what is not being used, so the neural connection of an old thought, if left unused for long enough, will eventually get pruned away. This is why you can't remember certain facts from 8th grade history class or the name of a former co-worker you just ran into at the grocery store.

Think of something you used to believe in very strongly but after getting some new information, you decided to change your belief. Santa is a good example here. The belief is so strong that parents can get their kids to go to bed on time or clean their room by playing the Santa card. The neural connection has been reinforced over time, and the recall is instant. Babies weren't born knowing about Santa; they had to learn by repetition. *It's the same exact thing with every other belief you have.* You had to learn it somewhere and then practice it for it to become automatic. The cool thing here is that if beliefs are learned, they can also be unlearned. If you have a belief that doesn't serve you, you can train your brain to believe in something new that does. Repetition is key here. Many ideas and phrases are repeated several times throughout this book *on purpose.* Repetition is how you will reprogram your thinking.

Your beliefs create the outcomes in your life. If you don't like what you are creating for yourself, then you have to train your brain to think new thoughts in the direction you want to go. Your brain is pliable, and it can be changed with practice. This is called neuralplasticity. As I mentioned before, your brain makes new neural connections when you choose to think new thoughts, and your brain can also prune away neural connections that are no longer being used (old thoughts that lead to bad habits that don't serve you). Once you come up with better thoughts to think, you must *practice* them in order for them to become a belief. Practicing your new, believable thoughts will strengthen the neural connections until they become automatic. You strengthen them even further by taking purposeful action to create evidence to support the new belief. This process is how you are going to rewire your brain.

Repetition is key here. Many ideas and phrases are repeated several times throughout this book *on purpose.* Repetition is how you will reprogram your thinking.

CHAPTER 17

THE WHY BEHIND YOUR WEIGHT

This is going to be a super juicy chapter! We are going to explore the reasons why you might be subconsciously choosing to wear extra weight on your body. It is important to fully understand *why* you're doing something before you can change it and let it go.

It may be hard to wrap your mind around this, but on some level you want your current results. How do you know? Because that's what you have. If you remember from the past two chapters, your mind is designed to create outcomes that match your beliefs. This goes for *everything* in your life, not just your weight. Your beliefs will drive which career you choose, your choice in whom you date, whom you marry, or why you remain single. The home you live in, the car you drive, the clothes you wear, and the amount of money in your bank account are all reflections of what you believe—and what you think you deserve.

Barring certain medical conditions, if you're carrying extra weight, it is on your body for a reason. It doesn't mean you're lazy and it doesn't mean you're a victim of it. Think of it another way— *the extra weight is there, doing a job.* How would the game change if you understood that you have hired the excess fat to do a job for you—that you are wearing it on purpose? Dig deep to find out what that job is; from there you can evaluate whether or not you continue to require its services. You will find that it's easier to let it go when you know why it's there in the first place.

I've worked with many, many clients over the years, and this is a collection of the main reasons why people hold on to extra weight. I invite you to read over them and see which ones resonate with you. It is common to have more than one reason, so don't be alarmed if you do. That's why it's called a *belief system*. Once you know what's driving your actions to keep the extra weight on your body, you can rework your thinking to change those neural connections. I've included some replacement thoughts with each belief to get you started in the rewiring process.

THE SILENT APOLOGY

This is when you use your weight to apologize for how great you are. You may have a lot going on for you, but if you think other people will find it threatening, you will wear extra weight to silently apologize for it. It's a way of saying, "See, I don't have it all. Look how I struggle with my weight." The weight you wear is the great equalizer.

Replacement Thoughts:
- I've worked hard for where I am, and I'm allowed to enjoy it.
- It's okay to appreciate how awesome I am.
- I don't dilute myself for the haters; I show up fully because I never know whom I might inspire today.

USING YOUR WEIGHT AS A WAY TO HIDE

This is when you use your weight to hide from the world. You let the extra weight take you out of the game. You don't have to be seen or try for what you want. By hiding yourself, you are also hiding your gifts. You're too busy focusing on your weight to be following your calling. Maybe you're afraid of failing, so you won't try at all. Or maybe you're afraid of succeeding because if you did, you'd be inviting attention to yourself and that feels terrifying to you. You use the extra weight as an excuse to stay close to home and out of sight. The extra weight makes you invisible somehow, even to yourself.

Replacement Thoughts:
- I'm beginning to see myself and how valuable I really am.
- I am one of a kind, and no one on this planet has what I have to offer.
- My contribution matters to someone out there, who can't receive it if I don't show up and make it available.

PROTECTION

This is when you use the extra weight as a physical barrier to protect you from being hurt. If you have experienced any form of sexual harassment or sexual abuse, wearing extra weight becomes a way to keep people away. It's either an actual physical barrier or you believe that if you make yourself unattractive, you will not attract unwanted attention. If you have not experienced sexual abuse but have experienced a broken heart, you may also be using extra weight to protect yourself. If you are not feeling your best, you will not enter the dating arena and risk your heart again. The ironic thing with this strategy is that you think the extra weight will insulate you and protect you from being hurt, but the reality is that you are hurting yourself daily with mean self-talk, overeating, and the pain of an unlived life.

Replacement Thoughts:
- What I experienced in the past is no longer happening now, but I keep reliving it every time I replay it in my own mind. I won't be doing that to myself anymore.
- I am strong, I am safe, and I'm able to stand up for myself.
- I am opening up to the idea of attracting love in my life again because I trust myself to make better decisions based on the lessons I've learned from my past.

SHUTTING DOWN YOUR SEXUALITY

This is a little different from using weight as a protection. This is more like being afraid of your sexual power. Maybe you were taught that it's not proper to be a sexual being or you were somehow shamed for being sexy. Maybe you think if you allowed yourself to be sexual, that you wouldn't be able to control yourself. I have worked with several clients who were afraid that if they lost weight, they would cheat on their husbands. One of my clients referred to the extra weight on her body as a "mojo-dimming coat." Here, the weight is used as a tool to control your sexual energy.

Replacement Thoughts:
- I'm becoming more and more comfortable being my sexy self.
- I don't need a layer of fat to keep me faithful; I am capable of making the right decisions for me.
- Being a sexual being is a natural and beautiful thing.

CONTINUING YOUR ROLE IN THE FAMILY

Were you referred to as the "fat sister" or the "husky one"? If you were given a label in your family, you may be unconsciously continuing to live out that role. I once had a client who was taught by her mother to never outshine her sister. Though her mother never specifically articulated it in this way, we uncovered that the role my client believed she was supposed to play was "the sister who dims her shine." This led her to engage in a constant struggle to lose those last ten pounds as an adult. She created a scenario in her mind that she wasn't good enough because of those last ten pounds, and she used the weight to keep herself from being the best she could be, as not to outshine her sister. This is how she maintained her (perceived) role in the family.

Replacement Thoughts:
- I am not the label I was directly or silently assigned in childhood.
- I do not have to continue playing this role in order to be loved.
- I get to choose who I want to be and how I show up in the world.

Using food as a substitution for joy

It's no secret that food can be fun. It can be very entertaining and can provide a lot of pleasure. However, when you are not creating joy in other ways, you run the risk of food becoming your sole source of joy. To be honest, it is only an illusion of joy because the sensation of eating delicious food lasts only a few minutes, but the weight you pile on from eating your joy can last for decades. This also goes for calling food your lover or your friend. If you think that food is your source of love or your only friend, it makes sense that you'd want to spend most of your time with it.

Replacement Thoughts:
- I am learning to find joy in many things that aren't food-related.
- I'm my own best friend, and I'm always a great influence on myself.
- Overeating isn't love, but taking good care of myself is.

All or Nothing Thinking

Many people who struggle with their weight are perfectionists. If you lean towards perfectionism, know that this kind of thinking will backfire on you because when you think you aren't being perfect with your healthy habits, you are likely to give up on them altogether. If you can't do something perfectly, there is this "Why bother?" attitude (for some of you, the phrase is "F*ck it!"), and you don't try at all.

Replacement Thoughts:
- Imperfect action is still action, and I'm good with that.
- Even the smallest effort will create results over time.
- I like the way I feel when I take care of myself.

YOU CREATE WHAT YOU THINK YOU DESERVE

Whatever you think you deserve, you will create a life that reflects that. If you don't think very highly of yourself, this may manifest in unfulfilling relationships, a dead-end job, and/or a body you're constantly at war with. Let's say on some level you believe you are inherently bad or wrong; you may think you deserve to punish yourself with overeating and a slew of self-directed insults. If you don't think you deserve better, then you'll never achieve more for yourself because your beliefs and your outcomes have to match. Even if you don't have low self-esteem, you still have a belief about what you think you deserve. Think about the times when you're just about to have a breakthrough or success and you end up sabotaging yourself. It's to bring you back down to the level you think you deserve.

Replacement Thoughts:
- Whenever I sabotage myself, it's a great opportunity to check in with myself and investigate why I'm blocking myself from having what I want.
- I've been mistaken about what I thought I deserved. It's time to raise the bar for myself!
- I am open to letting myself have more than I ever have before.

USING YOUR WEIGHT AS A DISTRACTION

As I've mentioned before, the weight struggle is a full-time job. It can be a very useful tool to keep you so busy that you don't have the time or the energy to pursue your dreams or develop an intimate relationship with yourself. Have you told yourself you will start a specific endeavor once you've lost the weight? Or maybe focusing so much on how you look on the outside is keeping you from ever having to look within? If you're afraid that what's on the inside is not good enough, then it makes sense that you would spend so much energy trying to appear good enough on the outside. The weight struggle is a great way to stay disconnected from yourself, never getting to know who you really are.

Replacement Thoughts:
- The more I focus inwardly and see how great I really am, my need to change the outside diminishes.
- I don't wait for perfect conditions anymore; I just get it done!
- Every day I get to know myself better, and I'm starting to see that I'm more than good enough.

USING YOUR WEIGHT AS A WAY TO REBEL

If you had a parent or caregiver who was hyper-focused on your appearance and you resented it, you may be overeating or carrying extra weight to rebel against them. Say they imposed certain food rules and restrictions on you as a child, but now that you are an adult, you could be overeating or choosing less healthy foods as a way to exercise your freedom of choice. In your mind, you think you are rebelling against your parent or caregiver (even if they are now deceased), but in reality you are only hurting yourself if you ultimately don't like the results your choices are leading to.

<u>Replacement Thoughts:</u>
- The opinions my parents/caregivers had of me were never about me; their opinions were always about *them*.
- I'm in charge of my choices now, and I choose to be healthy.
- I exercise my freedom of choice in ways that lead to the best outcomes for me.

WEIGHT LOSS AS A HOBBY

People like to do things they are good at. They create art, play sports, or may be very good cooks. Maybe over the years, you've become really good at dieting. Weight loss has become a hobby for you, like knitting, except the project you're working on is trying to make your body look a certain way instead of making a sweater or a scarf. You are an expert at planning your meals, charting out your workouts, and making friends at Weight Watchers meetings. You might actually like the anticipation leading up to the diet, the thrill of the big initial weight loss (usually water weight and muscle loss), and the excitement of the weekly weigh-in gamble. Is your weight up this week? Is your weight down? You might get hooked on the compliments you're beginning to get from other people. If you actually lost weight and kept it off, that would mean that the game would be over. For some of you, that would be terrifying because you'd lose the one thing you're really good at. If you think this way, you must sabotage yourself to keep the game going.

Replacement Thoughts:
- I am good at many things.
- I am open to trying out some new hobbies.
- There's way more to life than weight loss.

YOU BEGIN A HABIT FOR A REASON BUT CONTINUE AFTER THE REASON IS RESOLVED

A client hired me to help her stop the binging she was doing when she returned home from work. As we worked together, I learned that she used to travel for a really stressful job and would suppress her unpleasant feelings by binging in her hotel room at the end of a workday. Now that she had a new desk job, she was still binging at night. If you remember from the beliefs chapter, every time you repeat a thought, a myelin sheath wraps around the neural connection and makes it stronger. In this case, her routine of binging after work became automatic and that's why she was still doing it, even though she had changed jobs. This also happens sometimes with moms who struggle with losing weight after giving birth. They told themselves that they were "eating for two" during their pregnancy, but the behavior continues after the baby is born.

Replacement Thoughts:
- What I thought was working for me then is not working for me now.
- I don't need to binge eat/eat for two/skip workouts anymore.
- I am building new neural connections by practicing new habits that serve me better.

CLINGING TO THE FAMILIAR

Humans are creatures of habit. This could be partially attributed to all the strong neural connections we have cultivated in our brain over time. To change them would take some work, and it can be uncomfortable to learn something new at first. So to avoid feeling discomfort, you continue on with what you've been doing, no matter the results. Many people not only hold on to what makes them miserable but also fight to keep it for the sole reason that it is familiar. I once heard author Martha Beck say something at a conference that made me sit up in my seat with recognition: "Clinging to something unpleasant does not equal security." This can be applied to any area of your life from unfulfilling relationships to material possessions that leave you financially overextended, and of course, to the weight struggle.

Replacement Thoughts:
- Just because something is familiar doesn't mean it's good for me.
- I'm open to branching out and trying new things.
- I'm willing to experience a little bit of discomfort as I build new habits that make my life better.

FITTING IN

This one is a BIGGIE! No matter how evolved we are, at heart we are still primal beings with a very strong need to be connected to our tribe. If you were shunned by your tribe in the caveman days, you most certainly would have perished. For females especially, this directly translates to "fitting in." Could you be keeping the weight struggle in order to fit in? By creating a weight problem for yourself, you get to be a part of the conversation a lot of women are having when topics such as calories, bathing suit shopping, and thigh-gaps come up over coffee or cocktails. It's like belonging to a secret club with its own language. Your weight issue is your ticket in. It says, "I belong. I'm just like you." Really think about this though: Sometimes the price to fit in is hating ourselves.

<u>Replacement Thoughts:</u>
- If I have to hate on myself to fit in, then that's definitely not the tribe I want to belong to.
- I pick friends who enjoy having conversations about interesting things that have nothing to do with body size or weight.
- I attract awesome people because I am awesome myself.

GROUNDING FOR THE HIGHLY SENSITIVE PERSON

A Highly Sensitive Person (HSP) is someone who is sensitive to bright or flashing lights, loud noises, various odors, crowds, and negative energy. HSPs are also very intuitive and empathic and often take on the emotions of others in their presence. If you are an HSP, you might unconsciously carry extra weight as a way to ground your energy. You either eat large quantities of food and/or foods that take a lot of energy to process (excess sugar, starches, and fat). The consumption and processing of these kinds of food seems to dull the high vibrations you feel in your body. Though this reason is not necessarily belief-driven, you can learn to manage your energy in ways other than using food, and this change can shift your weight.

Replacement Thoughts:
- Instead of using food, I can ground my energy by standing barefoot on the earth, by burning some sage to clear my energy, or by taking a shower and letting the negative energy wash down the drain.
- I mentally project an imaginary energy shield around my body to protect myself if I'm going to be out in a crowd or if I am in the presence of someone who is negative.
- It's okay to retreat to restore my energy in a quiet space.

LIVING OUT BELIEFS PASSED ON TO YOU BY YOUR PARENTS OR CAREGIVERS

This directly relates to Chapter 4: You Don't Have to Live What You Learned. Below is a small list. Try to think about what you were taught that you still believe today.

Examples:
- Clean your plate/Don't waste food (This leads to overeating regardless of what your body says).
- Our whole family is fat, so you will always struggle with your weight (On a subconscious level you stay overweight so that you can fit in with your family).
- There's never enough (Scarcity thinking leads to overeating).

Replacement Thoughts:
- Guilt is not a reason to eat food I am not hungry for.
- I am not my family's story. I decide how healthy I want to be.
- I have enough right now, and if I get hungry again later, I can have more.

USING YOUR WEIGHT TO PROVE THE CORE BELIEF YOU HAVE ABOUT YOURSELF

When you believe something, you will seek or manufacture evidence to support your belief and prove it true.

"There's something wrong with me."—When you think this about yourself, then losing weight only to gain it right back again, sabotaging your weight loss efforts and staying stuck, or piling on more and more weight can be just some of the ways you prove to yourself that there is something wrong with you.

"I'll always be a disappointment."—You create a weight problem to keep you from living out your potential so that you can prove the belief that you're a disappointment.

"I'm not good enough."—This is the grandfather of core beliefs. Most every negative core belief boils down to this one thought. You think you're not lovable because you're not good enough. You're not as successful as you want to be because you think you're not good enough. You think that the extra weight you carry makes you not good enough, but I want to offer you the truth here: The belief that you're not good enough *came first*—and *then* you manufactured the extra weight as the evidence you can point to and say, "See? I'm not good enough. Here's my proof."

<u>Replacement Thoughts:</u>
- I'm open to being wrong about the core belief I've been holding onto.
- Just because I've believed something about myself for a long time doesn't make it true and doesn't mean that I have to

keep on believing it.

- I'm willing to begin seeing myself in a better light.

FIGURING OUT FAT'S JOB

Now that you've read through this list of reasons, you might have a better idea of why you are choosing to wear the excess weight. When you understand why you're choosing to wear it, you can then begin the process of taking it off. If you're still not quite sure what your reasons are, I invite you explore your mind by answering these questions:

1. The excess fat on my body provides _____ (protection, excuses, etc.).

2. The excess fat on my body helps me to _____ (hide, keep relationships at bay, etc.).

3. The excess fat on my body is like a _____ (shield, companion, etc.).

This process does not have to be so serious. A fun way to lighten up and add humor to this is to take your answers and write out the employment ad that the excess fat responded to before you hired it. Example:

WANTED: Stay-at-home Mom/Busy Executive/Egg Farmer (whatever) seeks a loyal employee who is available 24/7/365 to provide protection at all times and must be willing to take the fall for every time I choose to not move forward in my life. You must also be excellent at keeping my Best Self hidden, especially when there is the possibility of romance or advancement in my career, as I must be shielded from rejection at all times. Please be okay with lots of attention, as I will be focusing on you—A LOT—and not in a good way. No references required, just show up ready to work!

Once you have a clear picture of the job fat has been hired to do, you can then decide if you want to continue employing it or not. For some of you, that answer is currently YES; you're not mentally or emotionally ready and that's okay. Right now, it might feel scary to let go of the excess fat because then you must deal with the reasons why you hired it in the first place. Know that losing weight may not be the best place to focus your energy right now. Maybe your energy might be better spent on healing your current thoughts about a childhood trauma, or practicing trusting again, or freeing yourself from the fear of rejection. When you heal the emotional reason(s) for inviting the excess fat to reside on your body, you will notice that you no longer need its services and can gently let it go.

Be kind to the fat. It has been a loyal employee, and it has done everything you have asked it to do. When you have decided that you don't need it to continue doing its job anymore, I invite you to write a Goodbye Letter to the excess fat in your journal. Please don't dismiss this powerful exercise as silly, as it could change your life the way it changed mine and the lives of many clients I have coached. Tell the excess fat how much you have appreciated it for all it has done for you, explain to it why you no longer require its services, and wish it well. And then gently, lovingly say goodbye.

CHAPTER 18

HOW YOUR THOUGHTS CREATE YOUR REALITY

A thought is a merely a sentence in your mind. I wish they taught a class in school on how to manage your thinking because a lot of people have no idea that thoughts are things that can be changed. Like most people, you might be under the misconception that you are the thoughts you're thinking. If you think a thought like "I'm a loser" over and over, then you believe you must be and will act accordingly. What you may not know is that you don't have to believe everything you think! You get to decide what you want to believe and what you don't.

Thoughts are very powerful things. The way you think influences every choice you make and every action that you take. Author Brooke Castillo explains this concept thoroughly in her book, *Self-Coaching 101*. She has given me permission to share the Thought Model tool she created to help you understand how your current thinking is affecting your life and how you can come up with better-feeling thoughts that support your goals and dreams.

You may have heard the term, "Your thoughts create your reality." This is true and I will explain this by using the Thought Model, which looks like this:

C:

T:

F:

A:

R:

C = Circumstance. A circumstance is neutral, free from opinion, and can be proven in a court of law. Everyone must agree that it is true for it to be a circumstance. Example: You think your husband is a jerk for bringing home a package of cookies, but he would disagree. In this case, the neutral circumstance in the thought model I'm about to demonstrate is "Husband brought home cookies."

T = Thought. A thought is a sentence in your mind. It's your opinion or belief about the neutral circumstance. It's your interpretation—what you're making the circumstance mean. Example: "My husband is sabotaging me. He knows I can't control myself around cookies."

F = Feeling. A feeling is a physical vibration in your body caused by a thought. This can be felt anywhere in your body. Fear can be felt in the gut; anger can be felt in your jaw as you clench it; love can be felt in the chest area where your heart resides, etc. A feeling is described using only one to three words. If your explanation of a feeling becomes a full sentence, then you are describing a thought ("I feel like he is sabotaging me"—this is a thought, not a feeling). Examples of feelings are "frustrated" or "out of control." You feel out of control in the presence of cookies.

This feeling may present itself physically as an uncomfortable swirling sensation in your torso.

A = Action. The action (or non-action) you take is in response to the feeling you're experiencing. Example: Feeling out of control in the presence of cookies, you mow through the entire bag, leaving nothing but crumbs.

R = Result. A result is the outcome you've created with the action (or non-action) you took. Example: Ate the whole bag of cookies.

To use this tool, ask yourself these questions and then write each answer in the corresponding line within the Thought Model:

What is the circumstance I'm reacting to? Write your answer on the C line.

What is the thought I am thinking about the circumstance? (Sometimes asking "What am I making it mean" about the circumstance will help you clarify your thought). Write your answer on the T line.

How do I feel when I think this thought? Write your answer on the F line.

What is the action I take when I feel ____? Write your answer on the A line.

What is the result I get when I take that action? Write your answer on the R line.

When using the Thought Model tool, you'll plug in your answers like this:

C: Husband brought home cookies
T: I can't control myself around cookies
F: Out of control
A: Eat the entire bag
R: I ate all the cookies

Your thoughts always want to be proven true, so the outcome (Result) you create will always provide proof for the thought you're thinking. In this case, eating all the cookies provides proof for the thought "I can't control myself around cookies."

Using this tool is very empowering because when you can see that the actions you're taking are caused by your thinking and not by external circumstances, you can take charge of your mind and begin to choose thoughts that lead to the outcomes you want instead. For instance, by using the thought model in reverse, starting with the Result you want and working your way *up* the lines in the model, you can come up with thoughts that will support your desired result.

Ask yourself these questions:

What is the result I want? Write your answer on the R line.

What action would I need to take to create that result? Write your answer on the A line.

How would I need to feel to take that action? Write your answer on the F line.

What would I need to think in order to feel that way? Write your answer on the T line.

A Reverse Thought Model looks like this:

C: Husband brought home cookies
T: I can have cookies if I really want them, but I don't like the way they make me feel physically, so I'll choose to skip them this time
F: Peaceful
A: Easily choose to skip eating the whole bag of cookies
R: Peacefully co-exist with cookies in the house

Notice that the circumstance is still the same (Husband brought home cookies). What changed was the thought you chose to think about it. One thought makes you feel out of control; the other thought makes you feel peaceful. You then engage in completely different actions that will create completely different results. Master this and you can end emotional eating forever.

The rules of the Thought Model are simple: A *circumstance* can trigger your *thoughts*, which trigger your *feelings*, which drive your *actions*, which create your *results*—and your results provide evidence for the thoughts you were thinking.

Now, if you've been thinking a certain way, those neural connections are very strong, and telling yourself a new thought you simply don't believe will make your brain reject it. For example, when you tell yourself you're ugly all the time, it's impossible to make the leap to "I'm pretty." You can say it a thousand times, but your mind will follow it up with, "No you're not!" and reinforce the old belief of "I'm ugly." Have you wondered why some affirmations don't work? It's that cognitive dissonance again. Your mind cannot hold two opposing beliefs at the same time. It will favor the one you've used the most. Repeating affirmations you don't believe can backfire on you, so this is where the use of Thought Modifiers is essential.

A Thought Modifier is like training wheels for the new thought you want to practice. It helps you believe the new thought in baby steps until it gets stronger and takes over.

Examples of Thought Modifiers are:

- I'm open to…
- I'm willing to…
- I'm becoming a person who…
- I'm learning to…
- I'm in the process of…
- Maybe…*

*Maybe is a great modifier when a thought is especially stubborn because it can open the door to possibility. If you have a thought like, "I'll never lose this extra weight," try shifting it just a little to, "Maybe I can lose this extra weight." Maybe is a gentle way of creating the space for change when you've been set in your ways for a long time.

When you've been telling yourself for years that you cannot control yourself around cookies and then you try telling yourself that you can peacefully skip them, your brain may not easily buy it. Using Thought Modifiers would look like this:

- I'm open to feeling peaceful around cookies.
- I'm willing to believe that I can feel peaceful around cookies.
- I'm becoming a person who feels peaceful around cookies.
- I'm learning to feel peaceful around cookies.
- I'm in the process of changing my thinking so that I can feel peaceful around cookies.
- Maybe I can feel peaceful around cookies.

You always want to run any new thought through the "Bullsh*t Meter" in your mind to make sure it passes. You'll know which one of your new modified thoughts will work the best because it will be the one that feels the most true. As your new modified thought gets stronger, you can try practicing some of the other thoughts to work your way up the ladder to something eventually like, "It's easy for me to feel peaceful around cookies, and I can skip them if I want to, no problem." Don't worry if you can't think your way into feeling "happy" about a circumstance. If you can choose a new thought that will at least bring you to feeling neutral about it, you're golden. Sometimes feeling neutral is enough because you don't have to overeat to suppress the feeling of neutral.

You're reading this book because you want to learn how to feel better than you have been. Perhaps you used to think that weight loss was going to give you the great feelings you're after, but hopefully you're now realizing that you've been looking in the wrong place. You're learning that you don't obtain good feelings from a thing, a person, or the size of your body. Good feelings are created by the thoughts you choose to think in your mind, regardless of your circumstances.

Many thoughts swirl about in your mind each day. If you wake up with the same crappy thoughts you were thinking yesterday and you leave your mind unattended, you will make today just as crappy. If you purposely choose to think better thoughts, you will create better outcomes. I love having that option, don't you? So, which thoughts will you choose to entertain today? I invite you to keep the positive and discard the negative by gently saying "No thank you" to any thought that feels yucky. Positive thinking is very powerful. Never leave home without it!

If a thought you're thinking makes you feel terrible, you don't have to keep it. A thought is a sentence in your mind and sentences can be rewritten.

CHAPTER 19

FEELING YOUR FEELINGS

A feeling (also known as an emotion) is a physical vibration in your body caused by a thought. When you think a thought, you trigger a release of chemicals that can be felt in your body. For instance, when you think about how much you love someone, you might feel a warm sensation expanding in your chest area or maybe you're afraid to give a speech in front of a crowd and you feel a strong, unpleasant churning sensation in your abdomen when you think about it. These are just two of the kinds of physical vibrations I am talking about. There are many different feelings, and the vibrations of each one can manifest in different places within the body, depending on the person.

Some feelings are pleasant, and you want them to linger. Other times, the vibrations feel so uncomfortable that you want to make them go away or distract yourself from feeling them. If you don't know that it's your thoughts causing your feelings, you will look outside of yourself for the remedy. Eating, watching TV, spending money, having sex, drinking alcohol, overworking, and doing drugs are the most common distractions people use to avoid feeling their feelings. In this book, we're going to focus on how avoiding your feelings leads to emotional eating.

It's not uncommon to feel a sense of fear or uncertainty when thinking about actually feeling your feelings. If you've become an expert at suppressing them, you might be worried that if you even dare to feel what you're feeling, you might start crying and never stop, becoming a non-functioning mess all rolled up in ball on the floor. I totally felt this way, too, but as someone who has gone through this process and has come out on the other side, I want to tell you that it's the *anticipation of feeling your feelings* that feels terrible. When you remind yourself that feeling a feeling is nothing more than being present with a vibration in your body, you soon begin to realize how doable this is.

According to author and neuroanatomist Jill Bolte Taylor, the experience of an emotion lasts for only ninety seconds. This is the time it takes for your body to flush out the chemicals that are causing the sensations you are feeling. When you keep thinking painful thoughts over and over again, you are stringing together several waves of physical vibrations that are ninety seconds each. It feels like the emotional pain doesn't stop, but really you keep reigniting the waves with the thoughts and stories you are telling yourself in your mind. Of course, this feels awful, and that is why you head towards your emotional eating escape hatch.

Emotional eating works in a few ways. First, it's an immediate distraction. Your focus is diverted away from the vibrations in your body to the mechanical motions of bringing the food up to your mouth, chewing, and swallowing. Next, you might experience a replacement feeling of pleasure for a few moments as you taste the food you're eating. Then, as you start to fill your stomach, your ability to feel the vibrations lessens. Think of a crystal goblet. When you flick it, it vibrates and makes a sound. The fuller it gets, the less it can vibrate and the sound is dulled. You are the goblet, and the more food you overeat, the less you are able to feel your feelings. Lastly, you might become so disgusted with yourself for overeating that you are now busy scolding yourself, which again provides a distraction from the original feeling. Boy, that sure is a lot of work to avoid being present with a vibration in your body for ninety seconds, huh? We will be exploring more on how to end emotional eating in Chapter 29.

As you learn the skill of feeling your feelings, old thoughts are still going to pop up. There are very few people on this planet who can control every thought they think. I've been practicing this work for years, and I am certainly not free of negative thinking. I have learned how to identify it faster and respond better, though. Now when I feel an unpleasant sensation, I quickly ask, "What am I feeling?" Once I've named it, I can ask myself, "What am I thinking that's causing me to feel _____?" I can then evaluate the thought and decide if that's what I want to believe or not. Sometimes my thoughts are so ludicrous that I laugh out loud and say, "I don't believe that!" and they quickly dissipate. Sometimes there is some truth to the thoughts I'm thinking, so I get out my journal and I write about it. I may also do some thought models as outlined in Chapter 18 to turn my thoughts around to something that feels better.

Not every thought has to be turned around right away, however. Sometimes it's very powerful to sit with a newly uncovered negative thought or belief for a while and fully understand how thinking this way has affected your life. The acceptance you eventually come to will be the foundation upon which the changes you make going forward are built.

It's very helpful to name a feeling when practicing feeling a feeling. Remember that a feeling can be described in one to three words. If your description becomes a full sentence, then you are describing a thought, not a feeling. Though there are dozens of feelings that can be experienced, I have compiled a small list of the feelings I hear a lot in my coaching practice. Examples of one or two word descriptions of feelings look like this:

Negative Feelings: Lonely, angry, shook up, sad, hopeless, helpless, unmotivated, scared, worried, scarcity or lack, defeated, bored, annoyed, miserable, over-sensitive, inadequate, desperate, discouraged, uncertain, and depressed.

Positive Feelings: Loved, happy, at ease, confident, capable, motivated, peaceful, excited, energetic, abundant, vibrant, content, encouraged, hopeful, positive, competent, accomplished, optimistic, satisfied, enthusiastic, and powerful.

A note on anxiety: Anxiety is not really a feeling, but rather what you experience when you are trying to resist the actual feeling that is surfacing. When you don't want to acknowledge what's coming up for you, you will first try to suppress it internally and this creates tension as you push against the feeling. When that doesn't work, you'll turn to the external distractions that were outlined earlier in this chapter to suppress the unpleasant feelings for you (food, sex, spending, drinking, etc.).

You are likely to experience a range of feelings on any given day. How you feel is driven by the thoughts you are thinking. Try looking at the thoughts that surface as merely an invitation to a party. You can either choose to accept the invite and go with the thought or you can decline the invitation and say, "No, thank you. I do not want to think this thought right now." Each day you get to decide how you want to feel. How you felt yesterday does not have to be repeated—unless you felt AWESOME, of course!

Most people who want to lose weight are after the feelings they think weight loss will give them. Weight loss can't give you the feelings you want; only your mind can. You don't need to lose weight to feel amazing; you can cultivate those feelings *now*, independent of your weight. This is the secret to getting what you want. If you feel great now, you are more likely to do what it takes to create the outcomes you desire.

Feeling your feelings is nothing more than being present with a vibration in your body caused by a thought you're thinking.

CHAPTER 20

YOU ARE A POWERFUL CREATOR

Where the mind leads, the body will follow. Whatever you believe on the inside, you will manifest on the outside. Be careful what you say about yourself, as your subconscious mind is always listening and will set out to make it a reality for you.

"I'll never lose this weight."
"I'm so fat."
"I'm out of control."
"Nothing works for me."
"I don't deserve to be happy."

Saying things like this to yourself programs your mind to make it happen. The extra weight you carry provides evidence for a belief you currently have. Can you see how the result of extra pounds provides proof for each of these beliefs? What is the belief that's causing you to hold onto extra weight and *do you want to continue believing that?* Your mind is *powerful*, which means *you* are powerful. Program your mind for what you want instead.

When coming up with new thoughts to program into your brain, remember that it is always more effective to head towards something you want rather than running away from something you don't want. Shift the direction of your energy with your words. By changing "I have to shrink this fat body" to "I am creating a healthy and fit body," you are now moving *towards health* instead of *away from fat*. What you focus on you get more of, so if you are focusing on how fat your body is, then a fat body will be the result you will create, even if you tell yourself you want to make it smaller. If you focus on feeling healthy and fit, then that's the outcome you'll make sure you end up with. Check in with the thoughts you focus on the most and then decide if that's what you *want* to get more of. Some things, yes. Other things, not so much.

Using inspiring photographic images can be very powerful in helping you manifest the outcomes you desire, as they can be a source of motivation or simply lift your vibe when you look at them. *The better you feel, the better things you attract.* Pinterest.com is a great place to gather images and make vision boards to support your goals. If you're going to make a vision board for your health and fitness goals, I invite you to choose images with body types that reflect your own. My body is curvy, so I choose images that reflect my natural shape. It doesn't make sense to pick images with a body shape that is not genetically possible to achieve. Personally, I choose not to set myself up for disappointment like that. If your thoughts about an image make you feel worse about yourself, don't use it! You don't want anything on your vision board that trigger thoughts that will bring you down (Example: "I'll never look like that"). Consider choosing images that reflect how you want to *feel* rather than a particular "look." Images that represent strength, flexibility, vibrancy, peace, or whatever feelings you're after are the ones you want to see every day as you practice believing your dreams into being.

Besides being a powerful creator, you are also a powerful magnet always drawing things to you. Like attracts like, so you are attracting the same vibrational match that you give out to the world around you. When you look at your life, you can tell what you are putting out there by what you're getting back. If it's not what you want, then fine-tune the energy you are currently giving off and watch how quickly things shift for the better.

What do you most want to attract in your life? Whatever it is, you have to send it out *first*. Say you want to attract (create) a better body for yourself to live in; then you are going to have to take really good care of the one you've got right now to show that you will take care of the one that's on its way.

You get what you give. As a living magnet, what are you drawing into your experience? Peace? Drama? Abundance? Lack? Focusing on your problems only makes them bigger, but hey, the same concept also applies to your joys! What do you want more of? Problems or Joys? You're placing your order with the Universe whether you are conscious of it or not. Since how you think makes a difference, I invite you place your order with some thoughtful care.

CHAPTER 21

STEP INTO THE ENERGY OF WHO YOU WANT TO BE

As you embark on your journey towards becoming more of who you want to be, a helpful tool to succeed in this endeavor is adopting the mindset of the Future Self you desire to become. If you think like her, you will act like her, and in time, you will *become* her (if you happen to be a man reading this book, simply substitute *him* for *her* and *he* for *she* as you read this chapter).

I invite you to ask yourself this question: *"Who do I need to be in order to have the body and the life I want?"* You are essentially describing your Future Self—who she is, what she does, and most importantly, *how she thinks.*

You might be inclined to write out a to-do list rather than a description of a person. If you notice yourself doing this, check in and see how you feel when you read that list. Many people can feel quite overwhelmed, possibly resistant to change, or even downright rebellious—all of which are counter-productive.

What I am beginning to learn in my own life is that sometimes when I create a to-do list for personal change, I end up rebelling against it and sometimes doing the opposite. Ack! To stop this pattern, what I have been practicing lately is skipping the to-do list and instead thinking of the person I want to be and then emulating her by taking on her thoughts and actions. For this exercise, I'm inviting you to imagine your Future Self, but sometimes it's easier at first to think of a person outside of you to gain perspective on the exercise and then bring that lesson back and applying it to your Future Self. For example, think about someone you admire. What do you admire about her? What do you think her thoughts are that create the outcomes she has?

I'm thinking of a woman who lives in my town. I've never met her, but I've seen her at the Farmers Market and at the grocery store a handful of times. She's probably in her mid-fifties; her style is smart looking (even in jeans and a T-shirt), her makeup is natural, and she doesn't color her hair, yet she SHINES! And it's impossible to miss how much her very hot and much-younger boyfriend adores her and is always at her side. I watch them move about the produce stands; he, always touching the small of her back while carrying their shopping basket, and she, picking up pieces of fresh fruit & veggies and lifting them up to her nose to take in their aromas with sensual delight.

I FREAKING WANT TO BE LIKE HER!!!

... Or at least the story in my mind about her.

My story is that she genuinely likes herself, she is confident in her sense of style, she's sexy, she's sensual, she appreciates the abundance the Farmers Market has to offer, she takes good care of her body and purchases organic produce to fuel her body with, and she is undoubtedly attractive—magnetic even. I certainly can't take my eyes off of her and the way she moves in the world. If I could take a peek into her mind, I'm guessing these are the kind of thoughts I would find:

"I like who I am."
"I am worthy of my own good care."
"I dress in a way that pleases me."
"I feel sexy and my boyfriend adores that about me."
"I savor every second of my life."

Thinking the way she thinks and emulating what I imagine her choices and actions are feels very different from performing things on a to-do list to be like her. *Emulating her is like stepping into the energy of her.* That's what I invite you to do with your Future Self. Think about what you want for yourself (a slimmer body, mental freedom from the weight struggle, etc.). Now, think about *how you would think* and *how would you act* if you already had the very thing you say you want. From today forward, be *that* person!

Creating your healthiest body begins in your mind, not in the gym or on your plate. You know that phrase "I'll believe it when I see it"? Well, author Wayne Dyer has a quote that is more accurate: "I'll see it when I believe it." In order to achieve success with any goal, you must believe that the result you want is not only possible, but that it has already happened. You must think, feel and act like you are already your Future Self in order to align with her.

I like to see people succeed, so here is a very helpful tip: Your brain likes present tense and "I am" statements. In my coaching practice, "I want to" or "I will" are known as "Someday Thoughts" (someday I'll have this, someday I'll do that). Those kinds of thoughts will get you nowhere, because your mind is not set on how it's already happening right now. Let's give the brain what it likes instead, shall we?

"I want to be healthier" becomes *"I take very good care of my body."*

"I will exercise 5 times a week" becomes *"I am consistent with giving my body movement."*

"I want to wear nice clothes" becomes *"I like wearing nice clothes."*

"I will eat when I'm hungry and stop when I'm full" becomes *"I am connected to my body's cues and I like to honor them."*

Note: You can absolutely use the thought modifiers mentioned in Chapter 18 to make your new thoughts as believable as possible.

Notice that these thoughts are in the present tense as if this is what you already do. That's the key. Live your life as if you are already living in your healthy Future Body, and your current body will eventually catch up. How can it not, right? You'll be taking different actions than you are now, so you cannot help but end up with an entirely new result. No matter what you want to shift, be it your weight, your finances, your career, or your relationships, this tool will work with anything. Albert Einstein said that your imagination is your preview for life's coming attractions. What are you imagining into being? The distance between who you are and who you want to be is separated only by the thoughts you choose to think.

———————

Creating your healthiest body begins in your mind, not in the gym or on your plate.

———————

POWER THOUGHTS
FOR SECTION THREE

I am willing to change the beliefs that no longer serve me.

There's nothing wrong with me; I simply have some beliefs that need to be updated.

All beliefs are learned, which means they can also be unlearned.

Since I am choosing to wear the extra weight on my body, I can also choose to take it off.

I don't have to believe everything I think.

I am willing to feel in order to heal.

I get back what I give out, so I am mindful about my thoughts and actions.

I place my order with the Universe with thoughtful care.

I'm becoming a vibrational match to the things I want in my life in order to attract them to me.

I align with my Future Self by thinking, feeling, and acting like her now.

INNER WISDOM ACCESS QUESTIONS
FOR SECTION THREE

1. The thoughts I think most often about my weight, my body, or myself are...

2. What are some examples of things I used to believe that I don't anymore? (These do not have to be weight related; it's just to show you that you *can* change your mind about something you once believed.)

3. After reviewing the reasons outlined in Chapter 17, the jobs I've hired the extra weight I carry to do for me are...

4. Am I ready to release the extra weight on my body from the job(s) I've hired it to do? Why or why not?

5. If I were to write a loving Goodbye Letter to the extra weight on my body, what would I say? "Dear Fat, ..."

6. On my way to reaching my Wellbeing Weight, I want to feel: (confident, adventurous, sexy, etc.)

7. What thoughts would I need to think in order to feel that way now?

8. Like attracts like. What are the things in my life that I don't like and how have I been a vibration match to those things?

9. Like attracts like. What are the things in my life that I love, and how have I been a vibrational match to those things?

10. Who do I need to be in order to have the body and the life I want? (Describe your Future Self in detail. How does she dress? Who does she hang out with? What does she do with her time? How does she care for her body? What are the positive thoughts she thinks? What is magical about her? The more descriptive you are, the stronger your vision will be. The more you know about her, the easier it will be to step into the energy of her.)

SELF-LOVE PRACTICES
FOR WEEK THREE

- Continue making simple daily entries in your food journal. See if you can spot where your beliefs are affecting the way you're eating. Be compassionate with yourself as you explore. Log your thoughts in your journal.

- Choose at least one thought from the list of Power Thoughts to practice this week. Add in another one to practice if you feel ready to. If not, just stick with the one.

- Get to know the thoughts you are thinking by answering the Inner Wisdom Access Questions for Section Three in your journal. Understanding the way you think is the key to your personal transformation.

- Practice feeling your feelings by naming the feeling and being present in your body while you experience the physical sensations of the chemicals washing through (*Example: This is loneliness, and it feels like a hollowness in my chest area; This is embarrassment, and it feels like a quickening in my abdomen; This is boredom, and it feels dull and heavy on top of my shoulders*). Focus on being fascinated by what you notice and feel free to jot down some notes in your journal. With practice, you will become a pro at feeling your feelings and you will no longer need to resist or avoid them by using food or other distractions.

Having a healthy mind is just as important as having a healthy body. Be sure to spend equal energy on cultivating both.

Section Four

Renew Your Relationship with Yourself and Your Body

CHAPTER 22

CHANGE HOW YOU TALK TO YOURSELF

The shortcut to low self-esteem is berating yourself with mean self-talk. Whether you say it out loud or you silently think it in your head, insults hurt no matter how they are delivered. Do you even hear what you're saying to yourself every day? If you've been thinking with a Diet Mentality Mind, you might believe that you have to shame yourself into getting results, but beating yourself up with self-criticism and self-punishment never leads to health, happiness, and wellbeing.

How do you talk to yourself? If it's in a mean or critical way, understand that this is a learned habit. Children naturally like themselves until they are conditioned out of it by the messages they receive from their caregivers, authority figures (like teachers and sports coaches), peers, and/or the media. Someone or something taught you to stop liking yourself, and you've been practicing this habit ever since. For some of you, you've become like a bully towards yourself, dealing out hurtful remarks and putting down everything you do. You've been doing it so long that maybe you don't even notice it anymore. Your body and mind, however, register everything you say and think about yourself. If what you said to yourself appeared as words on your skin, would you be more aware of how you talked to yourself then?

Well, how you talk to yourself *is* showing up on your body, just not as words. It's showing up as the extra weight you carry. How you look on the outside is a manifestation of the way you talk to yourself on the inside. Luckily, this works both ways. Speaking kindly to yourself and offering yourself support and encouragement will reflect quite differently in your appearance and in your outlook on life as a whole.

The first step in stopping the self-shaming is to become aware of it. Start paying attention to what you're saying to yourself. It helps to note the insults in your journal—not to shame yourself even further but to actually see what you're saying so that you can change it. Have compassion with yourself during this process, as bullies are usually the ones who are the most in need of love.

Once you're aware of what you're saying, I invite you to stand up for yourself and defuse the insults immediately. Because of strong neural connections, the insults might be automatic for now, but that doesn't mean they can't be changed. Decide to be the hero in your own life. If bullying thoughts come up, step in and stop it. Practice saying something like, "I am not going to allow myself to talk to myself this way anymore." Follow up with saying something kind and supportive to yourself ("You're really trying and that's what matters" or "You can totally do this"). It takes some effort for any new habit to become effortless, and the more you practice this, the easier it gets. If you stick with it, there will come a day when you speak to yourself with such genuine kindness that when an inner insult surfaces, it will seem totally laughable and out of place.

No matter how long you've been engaging in mean self-talk, you can absolutely turn this behavior around. Make it your mission to stop the punishing thoughts and become your greatest cheerleader instead. Spending 24/7 with someone who is nice to you can make all the difference in the world. Let that person be YOU!

The shortcut to low self-esteem is berating yourself with mean self-talk. Make it your mission to stop the punishing thoughts and become your greatest cheerleader instead.

CHAPTER 23

BE YOUR OWN BEST FRIEND

If you haven't been treating yourself very well, you're probably not very good friends with yourself. Would you be friends with someone who called you names and made mean comments about your body? Yeah, didn't think so. Since you are going to be spending the rest of your life with yourself, it would make a huge difference if you treated yourself like you would your best friend. I know that sounds cliché, but living day after day with your worst enemy is its own special kind of hell, and you deserve way better than that.

Friendships take effort to cultivate and grow. First, you have to meet. For some of you, you will be meeting yourself for the first time during this journey. You've been living your life on autopilot driven by thoughts you've picked up from other people, and you have yet to uncover the real you. As with any friendship, there's that "getting to know you" stage. What do you like to do? How do you like to spend your time? What are the things in life you absolutely love? What are you good at? What are the things you'd like to learn? Getting to know yourself can be a fun time of discovery! Think about your best friends and what drew you to them. What was it about them that made you want to include them in your life? Like attracts like, so what are the awesome traits *you* have that your friends find attractive in you? Focus on those as you begin building your friendship with yourself.

Some of you already know yourselves pretty well, but you lack trust with yourself because you think you've made some mistakes in the past and let yourself down. Well, maybe you did make some choices that were driven by faulty thinking, but now you're learning a *new* way to think that will lead to better outcomes. Since you can't go back and change anything, do yourself a huge favor and forgive yourself. What you did way back when is not who you are today. You can have a fresh start anytime you decide to give yourself one. When you're ready, a great way to begin building self-trust is by following through with what you say. When you make a promise to yourself and you keep it, you begin to believe in yourself again. Your confidence grows when you know that you can rely on yourself and that you have your own back.

Moments on this journey are going to be challenging, and you are going to tell yourself that you want to quit. This is when you step in and encourage yourself to keep going. Remind yourself why you're making the effort in the first place and turn to yourself for the inspiration you need. Be your own support system. Like any best friend would, tell yourself things like, "You've got this! You're amazing, and I believe in you." Please do not pooh-pooh these inner pep talks. You're talking to yourself with your thoughts anyway, so you might as well be building yourself up instead of tearing yourself down.

We choose our friends for many different reasons, but mainly because we like how we feel when we are around them. Become someone you enjoy spending time with. Be fun, be interesting, play more, laugh more, and smile.

CHAPTER 24

IT'S OKAY TO LIKE YOURSELF

Even though we are inundated with messages to strive for beauty, success, and romantic love, actually celebrating ourselves and our achievements can often be frowned upon by the haters in this world. Heaven forbid you let it be known that you like yourself, only to be met with judgments:

"Conceited"
"Full of yourself"
"Stuck up"

No wonder we get conditioned to dislike ourselves! We want so badly to belong that we strive for what we are led to believe is culturally acceptable, but then we must downplay what is amazing about us to avoid criticism. This kind of faulty thinking is crazy-making, and it's in desperate need of an overhaul.

That it's wrong to like yourself is one of the worst limiting beliefs you could ever have, and it's definitely one worth questioning. Just because some people believe it doesn't mean you have to, too. There are plenty of people who believe the exact opposite, and they are actually pretty pleasant to be around. What makes people who like themselves so likeable?

- People who like themselves are genuinely nice to other people.
- People who like themselves know how to enjoy life and have fun.
- People who like themselves talk people up instead of talking them down.

Now that I think about it, the haters who think you are conceited or stuck up for celebrating yourself and liking who you are probably don't like *themselves* very much. It must be pretty painful for them to see someone else be happy when they are not. Maybe they would find you less threatening if you came down a peg or two, so they shame you for your awesomeness. Well, it's your life, and you can either cave in to their whims or you can keep feeling great about yourself and go out and seek better company (more on this in Chapter 46).

If you need help wrapping your mind around the concept of liking yourself or improving your self-esteem like I did, allow me to share a tool I created for myself when I was trying to figure this out. I used to hear the term "self-esteem" tossed around a lot in the self-help realm, but I never fully understood what it meant. Then one day I heard self-esteem described as "having a high opinion of yourself" and for someone who had developed a rather *low* opinion of herself over the years, it really was a light bulb moment for me. I began to think about the high opinion I held for many people in my life and then I thought about how I treat them:

- I treat them with respect.
- I give them extra attention.

- I speak highly of them to others.
- I wish the best for them.

It kind of stung to acknowledge how poorly I was treating myself in comparison to this list. If I wanted to treat myself better, I was going to have to think better of myself. If I held myself in high esteem, it was more likely that I would act accordingly:

- I would treat myself with respect.
- I would give myself extra attention instead of ignoring my own needs.
- I would speak highly of myself to myself and possibly others (or at least not bash myself or apologize for myself in front of others).
- I would wish the best for myself instead of telling myself that I can't have something because I wasn't worthy.

I invite you to make a list of the people in your life that you think very highly of. Next to their name, write down how you treat them. Do you notice a discrepancy between the way you treat them and the way you treat yourself? If so, consider making a practice out of treating yourself the same way you treat those whom you hold in high regard (as I illustrated in my own work above). Of course you are going to have to create the kind of thinking that will match your actions, so I'll start you off with two thoughts to get you on your way: "I'm open to believing that it's okay to like myself" and "Today I will act like I like myself." The second thought I especially like because it's a starting place to help you treat yourself better until it becomes a habit.

Know that it is not only okay to like who you are, but it is imperative for your long-term success. When you feel good about yourself, you are more likely to care for your body in a way that makes the weight struggle disappear. It is very hard to harm your body with overeating or any other self-defeating behavior when you like yourself.

It is not only okay to like who you are, but it is imperative for your long-term success.

CHAPTER 25

UNWIND MEDIA-DRIVEN PERFECTIONISM

It has been said that beauty is in the eye of the beholder. This is true; we all have our own definition of beauty, but we do so based on the beliefs we've been collecting since childhood. With the thousands of images filtering into our brains each day through films, TV, billboards, magazines, and the Internet, our beliefs about what is attractive have been shaped by what we see and what we have decided to believe about it.

The beauty industry would like us to believe that if we bought their products, our life would be enhanced in some way. They prey on our fears of not being good enough and offer us a remedy if we are willing to part with our money. Sometimes it seems like they invent a problem where there is none and then sell us something to fix it. I'll never forget how angry I felt when I saw an ad for a deodorant that contained a bleaching agent to lighten dark spots in your armpits. Seriously? Now we have to be worried about our armpits looking perfect? As if we haven't been given enough reasons to hate our bodies already.

Perfectionism is an insidious thing. We are conditioned to chase perfection to feel good about ourselves, but ironically it never delivers. It never delivers because it doesn't exist. Models go through hours of hair, make-up, and styling before posing under special lighting in front of the camera. This is all before the magic of photo retouching takes over. The images are so altered that the models don't even look like the doctored images in real life. Photo retouching has gotten so out of control these days that sometimes parts of the model's body are missing entirely, and you could drive a truck through the artificial space between her thighs. The images of "perfection" we end up seeing in the final product promote an ideal that is impossible for any human being to attain. I like to call these types of images "processed beauty." Processed beauty reminds me of all the processed foods that line our grocery aisles—the fake foods that make us ill when we consume them. When we consume the processed beauty that we see lining the magazine racks, we can make ourselves just as ill as consuming fake food. We need to remember that processed beauty is not real, especially when we're tempted to compare ourselves to the altered images we see. Think about this: We compare ourselves to images that aren't even real and then make ourselves wrong for not measuring up. Talk about the definition of self-abuse.

So many of the messages in magazines and in the media can be damaging to our self-esteem if we buy into them. We are told that natural occurrences such as body hair, stretch marks, acne, age spots, cellulite, wrinkles, gray hair, and teeth that aren't perfectly white are flaws that need to be fixed, covered up, or eliminated. Men have it bad as well, as the messages they receive are that they must be tall, free of body hair, ripped with muscles and six-pack abs, *and* be sporting a full head of hair. While we may not be able to completely avoid the messages offered to us, we *can* decide to let them affect us or not. Keep reminding yourself that the images of perfection in the media are created to sell products or services to make a profit. It wasn't all that long ago that the curvy Marilyn Monroe look was in and naturally thin women were subjected to ads to *gain* weight. All body types are lovely and worthy of celebration, not disdain. Would you treat your body better if you stopped comparing it to what you see in the media? My guess is YES.

Who you are at the center of your being is already amazing. Whenever you focus on your perceived imperfections, you block yourself from feeling true happiness. Your brain is so occupied with what you think is wrong that there's no room for feeling good about yourself. You don't have to think this way. YOU get to define you. Not a scale, not the phony airbrushed media standards, not other people's opinions. You get to decide how you want to see yourself, who you want to be in this world, and how you want to live in it. Be comfortable with who you are and focus your energy on being your best YOU. When you tell yourself the lie that you should be different or more like someone else, this sets you up for unnecessary struggle and emotional pain. Stop comparing and start celebrating the YOU that already exists. You're pretty awesome, you know.

We need to remember that processed beauty is not real, especially when we're tempted to compare ourselves to the altered images we see.

CHAPTER 26

LEARN TO LOVE THE BODY YOU LIVE IN

All people deserve to love their bodies, and all bodies deserve to be loved. Deep down, you want to love your body. Up until now, however, your love has been conditional based on how your body looked or how much it weighed, or both. Imagine loving your children based solely on their looks. Imagine your pet's weight determining whether you love it or not. Imagine accepting or rejecting your best friend depending on her dress size. This all sounds ridiculous, right? You don't love someone for their appearance; you love them because they are important to you. You feel grateful for their presence in your life, and you would miss them terribly if they were gone tomorrow. If you don't currently love your body, could the issue be that your body is not important enough to you or that you are not grateful for it? Consider for a moment all that your body does for you and see if that changes the way you feel about it.

No matter how you treat it and no matter how many mean things you say to it, your body still has your back, showing up to be your vehicle as each sun rises. It is a marvelous biological machine performing miraculous tasks for you every day without direction. Your body *wants* to be healthy. There are amazing processes going on at all times to keep it functioning. Your heart beats without your help; your food gets digested; oxygen is being processed; and many maladies that are going on within your body are being handled before you ever even know about it. Your body is constantly healing itself in spite of some of the choices you make. If you happen to overeat, it goes to work to process all the extra food you have just consumed. It processes the chemicals that appear on food labels, and it processes the chemicals you don't even know are there, like in the water you drink and in the air you breathe. Wouldn't you agree that all of these things are worthy of appreciation?

Since your body is constantly working to keep you healthy, a really good question to ask yourself is this: *What would happen if I didn't throw obstacles in its way?* Imagine the state of health you could enjoy if you made it easy for your body to do its job. A well-loved, well-cared for body is definitely a joy to live in, so consider being an ally to your body and help it along by giving it plenty of sleep, staying hydrated, eating fuel with life force in it, and maybe even offering your body some kindness and affection. When your body thrives, you thrive.

Though you may have thought otherwise at one time or another, your body has never been your enemy. It has always been your loyal companion and continues to be. How would things be different if you decided to treat your body as you would your closest friend? Think about what it would be like if you always wanted the best for it, kept it out of harm's way, spoke kindly to it, and delighted in its pleasure. Imagine trusting your body and imagine your body trusting you.

To build this kind of friendship with your body will require some vulnerability and intimacy. Intimacy is built with communication.

Your body is always communicating with you, but are you listening? Sit quietly and mentally scan your body, starting from your toes and going all the way up to the top of your head. Was there any part of your body asking for your attention? No? Are you sure? Slow down and try listening again. I have a feeling that your body is communicating to you right now and is waiting patiently for you to hear what it has to say. If your body could talk, what would it be asking you for right now? Nourishment? More sleep? Some movement? A hug? Once you hear the answer, I invite you to take action and respond to the request your body is making. Being there for your body the way it is there for you builds trust in the partnership you are going to have for the rest of your life.

Your body deserves to be healthy, no matter what it weighs. It is precious and it relies on you for its care. Loving your body is the only way you'll take care of it long-term. You would never feel motivated to take care of someone you hate or think is gross, but you would go to the ends of the earth for someone you love and cherish. Let your body be that someone. Just as you do not have to be thin to be lovable, neither does your body. It deserves to be loved just for being. It deserves to be loved *by you*.

CHAPTER 27

FOCUS ON YOUR WELLBEING INSTEAD OF YOUR WEIGHT

Every dieter has that magic number in her head that she thinks will solve all of her problems if it were to appear in the little window on the scale. Of course, a number on a scale has absolutely no power at all, except for the power we give it in our minds.

I once worked with a client who sought my help after regaining all the weight she lost while eating only yogurt and lettuce for an entire year. The diet she was using was obviously not sustainable long-term, and the immense deprivation triggered months of overeating. First, we worked on her mind to stop the binging and the self-sabotage. Next, I helped her design a livable lifestyle that included healthy eating and regular exercise. Because of the resistance training she added to her self-care routine, she built up lots of muscle, which made her leaner than ever before. She went down three full dress sizes and was astounded to be able to fit into the clothes she bought while on the restrictive diet the previous year, especially since she was about 45 pounds heavier than her lowest weight on that diet.

During one of her sessions, she began to upset herself with the story that she was still 130 pounds away from her goal weight. When I asked her why she wanted to weigh that particular number, she told me that her doctor once showed her a chart and told her that was what she should weigh. She had been carrying this belief around for years, constantly comparing herself against that number and beating herself up about "not being good enough." She admitted that this particular goal weight seemed so far away that she often thought, "Why bother?" and would want to binge in response to the hopelessness she created in her mind.

I reminded my client that with her current self-care routine, she was able to wear the same size as when she was strictly dieting with no exercise. Instead of a goal weight, I asked her what size clothes she wanted to wear. Her reply was only three sizes away from the size she was currently wearing. I said to her, "You're only three sizes away from where you want to be, so if you lost 130 more pounds, what would be left of you?" She was shocked. All this time she had been beating herself up about being so far away from the magical goal weight in her mind that it kept her from seeing how close she already was to living in the body she'd been wishing for. She expressed extreme relief to finally let go of that goal weight number and instead, chose to feel peaceful in her body while continuing on with her self-care routine. This new outlook led to her taking herself on her first vacation in years (the very vacation she'd been putting on hold until she was "thin"). While at the resort, she frolicked in the ocean waves, enjoyed her body as she swam in the hotel pool, savored the delicious flavors of the local fare, and treated herself to a piece of artwork that spoke to her soul. During her coaching session upon her return, she marveled at the fact that she could appreciate her body so much and that she did not need to weigh a certain number to do so. It was music to my ears.

When you live your life with a Wellbeing Mind, it becomes easier to treat your body better, your relationship with food becomes more peaceful, and your mind naturally begins to favor kind self-talk. With consistent self-care and the cessation of chronic emotional eating, the weight your body instinctively settles into is your "Wellbeing Weight." Know that this may or may not be the same as the magic number in your mind. Your body knows best and it will gravitate to the weight at which it functions most optimally. Allowing your body to choose its own weight involves the element of trust. In paraphrasing my colleague Lisa Hayes, let's imagine you are eating right and exercising regularly, you are loving your body every day, and you are living in gratitude for the gifts it gives you. Would you be willing to let your body decide what weight it wanted to be? Would you be willing to stop fighting with your body for those last few pounds and just do right by it, no matter what the scale says?

If you're like me and so many of my clients, you will come to value your wellbeing over a scale number any day. Here are some of the things I have heard my clients say:

"It is not about a number on a scale or a clothing size but how I want to live my life and who I want to be in the world—all of which I can already do in my current body."

"I have been focusing on creating awareness and connecting with myself for several weeks now. It's funny, I feel so good about myself that the number on the scale doesn't matter anymore."

"I went out last night and everyone complimented me and asked me how much weight I've lost. Funny thing is, I have yet to step foot on a scale and haven't been trying to lose weight. I've just been living my life the way I imagine my Future Self would. I love it!"

Instead of a scale weight, set your mind on how great you want to feel. And yes, what you end up creating for yourself might be different from what you originally had in mind, but who knows? It just might be a thousand times better! Know that it is possible to get to that place where your scale weight no longer matters to you. It won't matter because the feeling in your heart that you were ultimately seeking will be filled by the love you have for yourself.

When you live your life with a Wellbeing Mind it becomes easier to treat your body better, your relationship with food becomes more peaceful, and your mind naturally begins to favor kind self-talk.

POWER THOUGHTS
FOR SECTION FOUR

I am willing to speak kindly to myself.

I stand up to the mean thoughts that pop up in my mind.

I'm learning to follow through on the promises I make to myself.

It's okay to like myself.

I am open to noticing what's uniquely attractive about me.

Maybe I am more awesome than I realized.

I am in the process of building a loving partnership with my body.

I take great care of my body because when my body thrives, I thrive.

I can trust my body, and my body can trust me.

I always treat my body well, no matter what the scale says.

INNER WISDOM ACCESS QUESTIONS
FOR SECTION FOUR

1. If I had a mentor to help me on this journey, what would I want him or her to say to me to help me feel acknowledged, supported, and encouraged? (You can mentor yourself with your own inner wisdom, so the answers you come up for this question are the things you'll want to practice telling yourself. Cool, huh?)

2. What is the kindest thing I can say to myself today?

3. What are all of the reasons why my friends would say that I'm a great friend?

4. How can I apply my answers from the previous question to my friendship with myself?

5. How would I treat myself if I thought highly of myself?

6. What's pretty awesome about me already?

7. What are the things I appreciate my body for?

8. What are the specific things I can do to help my body thrive?

9. What is my definition of "Wellbeing" and what will it look like when I create it in my life?

10. If I woke up tomorrow morning and no longer used the scale number to determine my value, how would I live my life differently?

Self-Love Practices
For Week Four

- Since this week is all about loving yourself and your body, I invite you to practice eating the way you imagine people who love themselves would eat. Make each food choice from a place of love and see what you notice. Continue making daily entries in your food journal.

- Choose one thought from the list of Power Thoughts to practice this week. If another one really speaks to you, feel free to practice that one, too.

- Build and nurture your relationship with yourself and your body by answering the Inner Wisdom Access Questions for Section Four in your journal.

- Practice treating yourself like you are someone you love. Speak kindly to yourself, offer support and encouragement, and praise yourself for your efforts, no matter how small.

- Practice appreciating your body for all that it does for you. Show it love by taking good care of it. Feed your body nourishing food, take it for a walk in the fresh air and sunshine, dress it beautifully, and speak to it with affection and gratitude.

SECTION FIVE

REINVENT YOUR RELATIONSHIP WITH FOOD

CHAPTER 28

STOP DIETING

Giving up dieting is one of the main steps in creating peace with food. As primal beings, dieting puts loads of stress on the body. Severe calorie restriction is seen as famine, and your body's internal programming to survive will kick in. Your metabolism will slow down in order to preserve energy, and the signals to store fat get turned on. Without sufficient calories, your body will sacrifice valuable muscle tissue for the fuel it needs to function. Your brain becomes focused on taking in easily storable calories in the form of sugar, starches, and fat. You're not lying when you say that you start thinking about food all the time when you're on a diet. That is very real. So is the inevitable binge that follows. For every deprivation, there is an equal and opposite overeat. These survival processes are why so many people report that they ended up fatter after dieting than before they started. The body is very good at protecting itself, and it will do what it needs to do to keep you alive.

Dieting is synonymous with deprivation, and the most seasoned dieters have conditioned themselves into a pre-diet pattern of what I like to call *last chance eating, front-loading,* or *last meal syndrome.* It's the hoarding before the scarcity. It's the overindulging before the restriction. It's the harming of your body right before your attempt to heal it. I get the first two (been there, done that), but it's the third one that I find very sobering. For many people, especially as we age, losing weight becomes less about being thin and more about being healthy. So, if health is our goal, why would we hurt our bodies with overeating right before we begin the process of healing it? I'm guessing that old diet mentality tapes are still in play, especially if you have told yourself that you are going to have to restrict your eating. This pattern of self-sabotage can be the reason why some people remain overweight because they keep taking in an enormous load of excess food every time they get ready for the next diet. Since the resolve to diet tends to die out in a matter of days or weeks, what if you chose to skip dieting all together and decided to simply treat your body better instead? Just imagine the head start you'd have with the cessation of all those pre-diet binges.

For chronic dieters, dieting can become a way of life because they are afraid that if they don't control themselves in this way, they will gain even more weight. True, if you've been severely restricting your calories for a long time and you decide to switch to intuitive eating, there may be fluctuations in your weight as your body adjusts to the changes. This is normal and temporary. When you begin treating your body well by providing it with the nourishment it needs, and it is no longer receiving the message that you're in a state of famine, your body's survival mechanisms can relax. Your mind will drop its preoccupation with food, and your body can feel safe to release the extra weight because its needs are being met.

Do yourself a favor: ditch dieting forever and focus your energy on liking yourself and caring for your precious body instead. Liking yourself and harming yourself cannot happen at the same time. The two are totally different vibrations, and they simply don't match up. You can begin to take care of your health and avoid the backlash of deprivation by using a tool I call "Adding it in." Instead of cutting out foods like you would when dieting, I invite you to begin *adding in* fresh, healthy foods into your nutrition plan. Add in something new each day or every couple of days. In a matter of weeks, you will have crowded out the less healthy stuff without ever feeling deprived, and your body (and mind) will reap the benefits of being well-nourished.

Liking yourself and harming yourself
cannot happen at the same time.

CHAPTER 29

END EMOTIONAL EATING

Emotional eating is eating for any reason other than for physical hunger. Your body requires only a certain amount of fuel each day, and anything else consumed beyond that is driven by an emotion. The main reason why we emotionally eat is to *avoid feeling an emotion*. No matter how you try, you cannot truly make unpleasant feelings go away by overeating. You can suppress them for short spans of time, but this means that in order to not feel them, you have to keep eating. The result of this coping strategy ends up on your body as excess weight.

Every time you use food to numb emotional discomfort or pain, know that you are also blocking your ability to feel joy and happiness. I first learned this concept in 1988 from a humorous and wise teacher named Mr. Kennedy in Business 101. Decades later, I heard the same idea come up again in the work of Brené Brown, who tells us that we cannot selectively numb. When you eat to numb painful emotions, you simultaneously numb pleasant emotions, too. It was such an eye-opener to realize that the emotional eating I was doing to cope was also preventing me from feeling the happiness I was desperately seeking.

When emotions rise to the surface and you push them back down with food, you are missing the opportunity to heal what's behind those emotions. They come up so that you can work on releasing the cause—most commonly a negative story you are believing. Remind yourself, "I must feel in order to heal." If you notice yourself eating (or wanting to eat) when your body isn't hungry for fuel, be curious about it instead of getting mad at yourself. Ask yourself, "What's going on right now? What am I feeling?" Try to name it and then allow yourself to feel the feeling and let it pass. Remember that feeling a feeling is nothing more than being present with a physical vibration in your body (for a refresher, see Chapter 19). Trust me, it's not the scary thing you think it is. If you recall, a wave of emotion lasts only ninety seconds. You're totally capable of being present with your body for ninety seconds, right?

On occasion the urge to emotionally eat will feel very strong, and sometimes you might decide to just go with it. No biggie. No need get down on yourself. Right before you begin to eat, however, I invite you to practice telling yourself, "I'm going to eat instead of feel what I'm feeling in this moment." Yes, you'll still be emotionally eating, but at least you'll be aware of it, and awareness is the first step to creating a change. For many, this is a necessary step in the process of ending emotional eating.

When your body is not busy processing excess food, the vibrations of emotions can be felt very keenly. The best time to check in with yourself is BEFORE you overeat; however, there is still magic available to you even after you have overeaten. The very next time you overeat, get out your journal and pen and ask, "Overeat (or Binge), what are you trying to tell me?" I did this one Friday night a couple of years ago and the answer was a game-changer for me.

I went out to a fabulous dinner with one of my girlfriends, and we had the best time. We were treated like queens at the restaurant where we dined, and we were served a complimentary dessert plate with many bite-sized goodies to savor. Each one was delicious, and it was the final touch on a very memorable evening. I was barely through my front door upon returning home and the next thing I knew, I was gobbling up cold leftover food from the fridge. I already felt satisfied from dinner and now I was uncomfortably stuffed. I sat in the living room and began to cry, "Why did I just do that to myself?" Instead of spiraling down like I could have, I chose to get out my journal instead. I said, "Binge, what are you trying tell me?" After writing a few lines, the underlying belief showed up on the paper: *I can't have nice things.* This belief is not new. I have seen it come up before but more around material things. Ruining my great evening out with a big binge when I got home was now making more sense. If I believe I can't have nice things, then having a grand evening out with my friend does not match that belief. I had to ruin it in order for my belief and my outcome to match. What an awesome insight! Since I do not want my life to be run by the thought, "I can't have nice things," I had to work on changing it. I started with a modified thought of "I'm willing to let myself have nice things," and over time I have been able to build up my thinking to "I love having nice things." Besides being able to enjoy my time with friends now, this new belief ripples out to include other things like treating myself to more stylish clothes, keeping my car well maintained, and going on fun vacations. It turns out that binge was a gift in disguise, for I wouldn't have found that old limiting belief without it, and my life would not be as rich as it is today.

Every time you overeat, you have an opportunity to get to know yourself better. Every binge is a chance to heal. I invite you to look at each instance as a doorway into discovering the "why" behind the urge. Know that the reason is never outside of yourself. The reason why you overeat is always because of the thoughts you're thinking. Questioning your thoughts and feeling your feelings are practices worth mastering, as both will help you end the pattern of emotional eating for good.

When emotions rise to the surface, they come up so that you can work on releasing the cause—most commonly a negative story you are believing.

CHAPTER 30

TAKE THE CHARGE OFF OF FOOD

Tell me, what happens when you're told you can't have something? You want it even more, right? Telling yourself you shouldn't eat something only makes you fixate on it. Once you have the food in front of you, a sense of urgency seems to take over, and you gobble it up in record speed, never really tasting it. Unfortunately, there is no sense of satisfaction once the food is gone, but perhaps you might notice the lingering presence of guilt, remorse, or shame. Common questions you begin to ask yourself are "What's wrong with me?" or "Why can't I get it together?"

The Diet Industry has taught us phrases like "giving up" or "giving in" when it comes to taking care of our bodies. This implies that you are adopting a temporary regimen, one that has strict rules about what you can and cannot do and what you can and cannot eat. This also implies that you and your body cannot be trusted.

This is a lie.

You and your body are absolutely trustworthy when it comes to your own care. It's when you try to fit yourself into someone else's little box of restriction that you lose your way. No one else knows what your body wants and needs more than you do.

If you feel like you have lost the ability to trust yourself (a common fallout of the diet war), I invite you to begin re-establishing trust with yourself by first giving yourself a break. Stop restricting yourself because deprivation is the quickest way to a binge. I can already hear your resistant thoughts: "But Suyin, if I let myself eat what I want, then I am sure to lose all control." To that I say, "Trust me." And more importantly I say, "Trust yourself."

A great example of how this works was when I was coaching a client on her habit of binging on the snack foods she bought for her kids. I asked her why she didn't buy snacks for herself, and she told me it was because she wouldn't be able to control herself around the food. Interesting, right? She wouldn't allow herself to buy what she wanted for herself, but she ended up binging on her kids' snack foods out of deprivation. She had to laugh at herself when she saw that she was binging in an out-of-control way anyway, even though her strategy was designed to keep her from binging.

To remedy this, I invited her to give herself *full permission* to go to the grocery store and buy anything she wanted. She balked at first, but I insisted that she trust herself. She emailed me twice from the store, feeling almost gleeful as she described what she put into her basket. When I talked to her on our next session, she was surprised at the report she had for me. Though she bought chips, cookies, and candy, she ate very little of it, and nearly full bags were still sitting in her pantry almost a week later. She couldn't understand it. I explained to her that by allowing herself to have anything she wanted, she took the charge off of the food by lifting the restriction and their forbidden-ness had lost their appeal. Interestingly, she found that she didn't even like the treats she bought after she sat down and really tasted them. She wanted those items only because she told herself she couldn't have them. Once she allowed herself the gift of choice, the charge was lifted, and she felt free around food, including the snacks she bought for her kids. To her amazement, this shift happened within one week.

What if you allowed yourself to have what you wanted? Savoring fun food is not only okay in the *Love Yourself Lighter* method; it is encouraged. When you let yourself have food you enjoy and learn to be present with it and truly taste it, it loses all of the power you were giving it. Give it a try. Get an empty basket at the market and walk every aisle of the store, giving yourself permission to buy anything you want. You may need to try this a couple of times to practice lifting old beliefs about control and restriction, but learning to trust yourself is worth the effort.

Sometimes just giving yourself permission to buy what you want is enough to take the charge off of food, but other times you may need to provide yourself with the experience of eating it guilt-free. You may find that the foods you once thought you loved really don't taste that good or you discover that fatty, sugary, overly salty foods feel terrible in your body, and you naturally get to the place where you don't want to eat them anymore (or at least not very often). When this happens, the decision to not buy or not eat certain foods is no longer made out of restriction or deprivation, but it is truly made from the place of self-love and a deep desire to care for your body. This is how freedom around food is created.

CHAPTER 31

FOOD IS MEANT TO BE ENJOYED

How often do you get to the end of your meal and can't even recall the experience? Do you settle for bland-tasting food because anything with actual flavor seems to be on the no-no list? How many times have you eaten food you don't like just because you read somewhere that it's supposed to be healthy? Healthy food is only as good as it tastes. If it's not delicious—and especially if it tastes gross to you—why bother putting it into your body? Unless you are extremely hungry and there are no other food options available at the moment, eating food you don't enjoy does absolutely nothing for your wellbeing. When you eat without awareness and then add the lack of actual enjoyment into the mix, you are often left feeling hungry for more. Contrary to the message conveyed by most boring diet plans, you deserve to enjoy the food you're eating. By that I mean *really* enjoy it. Food that is followed by guilt and remorse after you eat it does not count as "enjoyable." True joy is never followed by crappy feelings.

Though it seems like common sense, this next advice is something that even I need to be reminded of whenever I read an article about the latest super food rage: Eating should never feel like punishment. I have tried on multiple occasions to drink organic apple cider vinegar water for it's reported health benefits, and I physically shudder as I try to get it down. I have tried to eat canned oysters for the zinc they contain and had to swallow them with my nose pinched. Thank goodness I bought only one can; that was the first and last I will ever buy. The worst was trying to eat organ meats after hearing over and over how good they are for us. Even cooking them in grass-fed butter was not enough to help me get past the first chew. I gagged before spitting that tiny piece into a napkin. Obviously, these are my reactions to these foods. You may have a very different experience, but any time the mere act of eating something stresses you out, I can only imagine that any possible health benefits become nullified as you try to digest in a stressed state.

Your body is valuable, and you want the food that you put into it to be worthy. Before you choose your next meal or snack, stop and ask yourself, "Do I even like this?" If you don't like something, don't make yourself eat or drink it! That goes for things that might start out delicious but then change in value the longer they sit. Take French fries, for example. They are wonderful when they are hot and crispy, but once they get cold, they can become soggy and you can begin to feel the grease coating your teeth and tongue. I do like to order fries on occasion, but as soon as they are no longer hot, I don't bother. My thinking about food is this: "If it's not worthy, then don't put it in your body."

To gauge a food's worthiness, I invite you to rate it on a scale from 1 to 10 (1 being gag-able, 5 being just okay, and 10 being utterly delicious and satisfying). Ask yourself these questions, too:

Is this enjoyable?
Does it taste great?

Do I enjoy the aroma? The texture? The temperature?

If it's not near a 10 on the worthiness scale, consider skipping it in favor for something that is. In other words, don't eat something that is mediocre only to then eat what you really wanted on top of it. When you eat food that you actually like eating, you nourish more than just your body. Food is one of the great pleasures in life that many Diet Mentality thinkers miss out on. They ruin the experience for themselves with deprivation, guilt, or eating so fast that they never even taste it. Food is not wrong and neither are you for enjoying it. When you slow down and allow yourself to savor what you're eating, your body and brain can feel satisfied, thus reducing the drive to overeat.

Eating should never feel like punishment. Food is not wrong, and neither are you for enjoying it.

CHAPTER 32

WASTE IT OR WEAR IT

The idea of wasting food can bring up extreme resistance in anyone with a scarcity mindset. Sure, it is programmed in our primal brains that food equals sustaining life, but in our modern world of relative abundance, the scarcity mindset had to be programmed into our brains by our caregivers or by societal messages during our childhood development.

Do any of these thoughts sound familiar?

- *"Clean your plate. Other people in this world are starving."*
- *"Food is expensive. You can't throw that away."*
- *"It's a shame to waste that."*

Do any of these actions sound familiar?

- Eating the discards off your kids' plates (pizza crusts, half a chicken nugget, two bites of an abandoned PB&J, etc.).
- Eating something you don't like the taste of simply because you paid for it.
- Eating the whole sandwich when you were already physically satisfied with half.

Our bodies require fuel to function but only so much at a time. It sends out signals that you're full for now and can stop eating. If you have a belief system in place about not wasting food and there is still food on your plate when you're already full, you're going to override your body's natural signals and keep on eating until the food is gone. You have now overeaten, and your body has to process more fuel than it needed. The excess food that's not being used to run your body will get converted to fat and into your fat cells it goes. Being unwilling to waste food can be a big reason why people hold on to extra weight.

When you are unwilling to waste food, also consider the other things that may be getting "wasted." Think of the time you waste putting your life on hold until you are thin. Think of the unworn clothes that are wasted just sitting in your closet because they don't fit. Think of the wasted opportunities to engage in pleasure and fun because you don't like the way you feel about yourself. Is eating excess food your body doesn't need really a good enough trade-off for these things I've mentioned? You may decide that it's not when you begin looking at it this way.

If you want to start shifting your beliefs around wasting food but are noticing resistance, please know that I understand. I was raised by a grandmother who raised her four children during The Great Depression, so I was definitely indoctrinated into a scarcity mindset where food is concerned. To be honest, I still don't like wasting food, but I've grown to love my body more, so I choose to work with the belief instead of trying to resist it. For instance, when I go to a restaurant, I check in with my body to see how hungry I am, and I'll order according to my hunger level. If I'm not that hungry, I will probably order a yummy appetizer and a bowl of soup or leafy salad. If there's an entrée I really want, then I'll order just that and eat until my body tells me it's full. I will have the rest wrapped up to take home to eat later when I'm hungry again. This is a great practice to adopt if one of your thoughts is, "I want to eat it all," even after your body says it's full (like a whole sandwich or a pizza). You can still eat all of it if you really want to, just not all at once.

People who also don't like to waste money will eat food they are no longer hungry for or eat food they don't even like simply because they paid for it. I understand this way of thinking, too, because this was totally me, and I still have to pay attention to the thoughts that pop up in my head sometimes. Recently, I bought a new item at the grocery store, tried it, and did not love it. For a split second, I contemplated finishing up the package because I had paid for it. Then I realized that I was not saving money by eating something I didn't enjoy. My body is not a garbage disposal, and it is worth more than $4.99. Into the trash the item went, and I felt awesome about honoring my body this way.

When it comes to overeating in a restaurant because you paid for it, a coach I know named Donna Kramer shared the thought she uses that makes it easy for her to let the waiter take away her plate of uneaten food: "I'm paying to be satisfied, and I've already gotten my money's worth." Wow! I love this thought because when you think this way and then follow through, you're showing yourself that your health is worth more than whatever ends up in the trash instead of on your body.

Each time your body tells you that it's full and you still have food on your plate, there are three containers the excess food can go into:

1. The fridge
2. The garbage can
3. The fat stores on your body.

You get to choose which container the food will go in. A simple mantra to help you make your choice each and every time is "WASTE IT OR WEAR IT." When you picture yourself wearing the excess food on your belly, on your thighs, your upper arms, or your butt, it kind of puts it in perspective. Know that wearing the excess food as fat on your body does not have to be your outcome. Know, too, that wasting food is always okay, especially if it means that you are taking care of your body by doing so.

CHAPTER 33

THINK BEFORE YOU EAT

You know by now that your thoughts drive your actions, right? Since this is always happening whether you are aware of it or not, it's important to take the time to find out what you are thinking right before you make the choice to eat. You are creating a result with each action you take, and your actions are cumulative. You might think that you engage in mindless eating but know that there is *always* a thought that caused you to pick up that bag of chips or carton of ice cream in the first place. Even the healthiest food on the planet can cause you to gain weight or remain overweight if you are overeating it. The key to change is catching the thought right before you eat and deciding if that's a good enough reason to eat or not.

I was working with a client who felt frustrated at the fact that even though she was eating healthy food, she was still struggling with her weight. She had been keeping a food journal, so we took a look at what she had eaten in the last 24 hours. I asked her to recall the thoughts in her mind prior to consuming each item in her journal entry. It looked something like this:

I love this morning ritual.
7:00 am Coffee with cream and sugar

I'm so hungry!
8:00 am Scrambled egg whites with veggies and plain toast

I need a pick-me-up.
9:30 am Coffee with cream and sugar

I don't want to answer this email.
9:40 am 1 protein bar

I'm hungry.
12:30 pm ½ turkey sandwich, side salad, iced tea

I'm bored.
2:50 pm 2 handfuls of organic raw trail mix

I want something cold.
4:30 pm Fruit smoothie

It's dinner time.
6:30 pm Chicken burrito, diet soda

I deserve a treat.
8:45 pm Organic popcorn

What do you notice about my client's thoughts in her food journal? Only *twice* did she eat because her body told her it was hungry. Every other thing she consumed was driven by a thought other than true physical hunger. She was taking in more fuel than her body needed, and since this was a regular pattern of hers, that's why she was holding on to the extra weight. For her homework, I invited her to pay attention to the thoughts she was thinking just before she reached for something to eat or drink, and if the thought was not, "I'm physically hungry/thirsty," then she agreed that she would practice skipping it until she was. It took her about two weeks to get the hang of it, but soon enough it became a new habit, and her weight began to shift.

What thoughts are driving you to consume what you do in a day? Aren't you super curious now? I invite you to begin listening to what you are telling yourself right before you eat or drink anything. If you are already keeping a food journal, consider jotting down your thoughts, too. The data you collect will likely surprise you. When you really see what your inner dialogue is and then you tie in the results you are creating with it, you might decide that it's time to change up the script! Becoming fully aware of the thoughts you're thinking but then deciding to take a different action can be one of the most life-changing, body-changing things you'll ever do.

CHAPTER 34

PEACEFUL EATING AT PARTIES AND HOLIDAYS

Virtually every holiday on the calendar is celebrated with an abundance of food and drink. At parties of any kind, be it dinners, BBQ's, weddings, etc., you will likely be surrounded by an array of yummy food items that you don't usually have at home. If you think with a Diet Mentality Mind, the thoughts swirling about in your head might sound like this:

"I shouldn't eat that."
"I can't eat that."
"I only get this once a year."
"That has too many calories."
"I've totally blown it."
"I'll start my diet tomorrow."

Social gatherings can also be fraught with emotions, obsessive thoughts, and anxiety, especially when family dynamics are thrown into the mix. Do you revert back to how you felt as a child with one disapproving look from your mother? Do you overeat to distract yourself from the drama unfolding at the dinner table with your in-laws? Do you load up your plate with more food than you need out of fear that once your siblings get to it, there will be none left? The Diet Mentality Mind is a fearful mind, and it causes us to abandon rational thinking. I want to offer you some helpful ways to navigate holiday parties and social events with a Wellbeing Mind so that you can feel peaceful, free around food, and cared for—all at the same time.

First off, I invite you to skip the diet tip that you'll find in any women's magazine at the supermarket check-out line that tells you to eat an apple and a drink a glass of water before going to a party to keep yourself from eating while *at* the party. When you do that, it's highly likely that you'll feel deprived in the presence of scrumptious food, and you'll end up overeating. A client of mine had followed the apple & water diet tip before going to a holiday office party and then spent the evening gorging on hors d'oeuvres. She was so upset with herself and felt shame about what she described as her "lack of control." I asked her, "What would happen if you went to the party with an appetite, tried a bit of each item that truly appealed to you and considered that your meal?" She hesitated for a moment while she contemplated the idea and said, "Gosh, I didn't know that was even an option." She tried it at the next holiday party she went to and was astonished to find how easy it was to enjoy herself and not overeat.

It is no surprise to hear that all-or-nothing thinking is a hallmark of the Diet Mentality Mind, especially when it comes to party food. When you tell yourself you can't have certain foods or you shouldn't eat them, you put a charge on them, begin to fixate on them, and end up eating way more, including stuff you don't even like. You overeat out of rebellion due to self-imposed deprivation, no matter how crummy it makes you feel. Do yourself a huge favor and take the charge off of food by telling yourself that you can have it if you want it. You can then decide if you really want it or if you are only wanting to eat it because you're telling yourself it's forbidden.

Another way to put a charge on food is to tell yourself, "I can only get this once a year." This thought drives overeating by creating a sense of scarcity. Another option is to create the feeling of calm by telling yourself the truth: "I can have this anytime of the year." Yes, you may have to make it, buy it, or ask your family member for the recipe, but you *can* have it any time you want it. Knowing that it's not scarce, you are less likely to feel the need to hoard it on your plate (and eventually in your fat stores). When you're feeling relaxed, you can choose items based on your desire for health and not from that scarcity place that makes you want to eat just because it's there. This way you can savor your favorites and simply leave the rest.

Speaking of savoring, during the holidays when goodies abound, allow yourself to have some of your absolute favorites and then slow down as you eat them so that you can actually *taste them*. Don't scarf it down as if to get rid of the evidence. When you do that, you rob yourself of actually experiencing what you're eating. I encourage you to free yourself of fear and shame about eating delicious food during a celebration. It's okay to enjoy what you eat. Really taste it, savor it, and by all means skip foods you don't absolutely love. Give yourself the freedom to eat until your body is satisfied, knowing that you can always go back for more later when your body tells you it's hungry again.

It takes only a moment to check in with your body while at a party. Are you hungry? Are you not hungry? If you notice that you are not hungry and you're about to sit down to eat with your friends or your family just so that you can connect with them, remind yourself that eating isn't connecting—connecting is connecting. You can still connect with your friends and family without abandoning your self-care. A simple, "No, thank you. I'm not hungry right now" is all you need to say to anyone who is pushing food or drinks upon you. Chances are they could be feeling uncomfortable about their own consumption and if you are eating and drinking, too, they may feel like that gives them permission to indulge themselves. Don't ever sacrifice your wellbeing to ease someone else's emotions. Yes, even the hostess who worked so hard to prepare the meal you're eating. It's perfectly acceptable to express your appreciation and gratitude with words, instead of with an empty plate and an uncomfortably full stomach.

Parties, celebrations, and holiday feasts are meant to be enjoyed. They are not meant to be an endurance test. At each social event you attend throughout the year, I invite you to bring your Wellbeing Mind with you. Allow your experience to expand way beyond the food that's being served. Take in the details of your surroundings using all of your senses; be present and engaged with the people you are spending time with; and laugh as much as you can. You always have the option of practicing happiness or practicing misery wherever you go. Whichever one you choose is what your memories will be made of.

Give yourself the freedom to eat until your body is satisfied. Know that you can always go back for more later when your body tells you it's hungry again.

POWER THOUGHTS
FOR SECTION FIVE

I am open to adding in healthy new foods a couple of times a week.

I am willing to let myself feel in order to heal.

Every time I overeat, I am given an invitation to explore my thinking.

It's okay to enjoy the food I eat, and it's okay to pass on the food I dislike.

I'd rather waste food than wear it.

My health is worth more than the cost of any food I don't like or I'm no longer hungry for.

I practice checking in with my thoughts before I eat or drink something.

The thought I want to be thinking most often before I eat something is, "I'm physically hungry."

It's becoming easier to say, "No, thank you" to food when I'm not hungry.

I am learning that I can enjoy the company of others without eating food I'm not hungry for.

INNER WISDOM ACCESS QUESTIONS
FOR SECTION FIVE

1. What are some healthy foods I want to try adding into my meals over the next several weeks?

2. When I think about having freedom around food, this is what I imagine it would look like:

3. Binge, what are you here to teach me? What do you want me to know?

4. What are the foods I've been telling myself I can't have that I'm now willing to experiment with by slowing down and actually tasting each and every bite?

5. What are the foods I'm making myself eat but don't really like? Is the reason behind my choice to eat it in the first place a good enough reason to continue?

6. What are my beliefs about wasting food? Am I willing to change them? If not, how can I keep my beliefs *and* take care of my body at the same time?

7. What are some of the main thoughts I'm thinking right before I eat (or drink) something? (I want a treat, this little bit won't hurt me, I'll start my diet tomorrow, etc.)

8. Are these thoughts serving me? Why or why not?

9. What are my current thoughts about eating food at parties and holidays?

10. What would I like my thoughts to be about eating food at parties and holidays?

SELF-LOVE PRACTICES
FOR WEEK FIVE

- Continue making daily entries in your food journal. Add in the awareness tool as described below.

- Choose at least one thought from the list of Power Thoughts to practice this week.

- Reinvent your relationship with food by answering the Inner Wisdom Access Questions for Section Five in your journal.

- Practice checking in with your thoughts right before you eat or drink something to build awareness of what's driving you to put it in your mouth. Is it an emotion? Or is it physical hunger? I invite you to write down the thoughts you're thinking above the meal or snack you log into your food journal so that you can begin to see the patterns that are contributing to the results you are creating (see Chapter 33 for an example).

Set your mind on loving yourself so much
that taking great care of your body is just
something you naturally do.

SECTION SIX

LET YOUR BODY LEAD

CHAPTER 35

GET REALLY GOOD AT BODY LISTENING

We all had it at one time in our lives before our primary caregivers' influence, before diets, before self-loathing set in. Actually, we still have it—we just don't know we have it because we haven't used it in a long, long time. What is it? It's our inner connection—the ability to hear what our bodies are telling us.

We were all born with this inner communication system and used it freely as children. It lets us know when our body needs fuel, when it's had enough to eat, when it's thirsty, when it wants to move, when it requires rest, when it is too hot or too cold, and when it's feeling ill. Most of us override at least one or more of these signals, giving various excuses like being too busy, having to meet a deadline, or thinking that we must put everyone else's needs before our own self-care. The result is a lack of energy at best, chronic illness or depression at worst.

In my coaching practice, I help my clients reestablish the connection that is already there. We start with basic hunger and fullness cues, then move on to Body Listening—tuning in to what your body is really asking for. Notice I said *body*. Some people will make the mistake of listening to their *mind*s, which often speak much louder than their bodies. Trust me, your body does not want brownies and potato chips for breakfast! Listen a little more closely. Your body might be calling out for specific nutrients by asking for certain foods. Have you ever noticed that you were fixated on a particular food—like a spinach salad or a juicy hamburger—and wanted to eat the same thing several days in a row, but then all of a sudden, you don't want it anymore? Your body stopped asking for it because it got what it needed.

Your inner communication system goes beyond the care and feeding of your body. You have the ability to tune in to the subtle energies of your environment and the energy of the people around you. You know when you meet people and you are instantly drawn to them? You sense their good energy, and it's attractive to be around. Conversely, have you ever met someone and immediately wanted to move away from him or her? You sensed bad vibes, even if the person smiled while shaking your hand. You can't explain it, but you can't help but tell yourself, "He/she rubbed me the wrong way." This is your intuition talking.

Your body is a living, breathing compass. No matter how you may try to lie to yourself about certain things in your life, your body always knows the truth. It will give you instant feedback when it hears you lie, but if you don't want to acknowledge the truth, you will tune it out. Chronic overeating may have turned down the volume of your inner voice, and you may have reduced your capacity to hear what your body is telling you from years of ignoring yourself, but you haven't lost the connection altogether. It's still there, and you can restore it by paying attention to yourself and listening to the messages your body is offering to you daily. Once you identify what your body is asking of you, you can then follow through with honoring your body's requests. The more you practice, the more the connection grows within and the more self-trust is established and strengthened. When you let your body lead, you no longer have to spend so much energy trying to control it, and your mind is free to pursue other activities that will enrich and enhance your life experience.

CHAPTER 36

HONOR YOUR HUNGER AND FULLNESS CUES

You are born with a perfectly-designed operating system that includes internal hunger and fullness regulators. When your fuel tank gets low, your body sends out signals that it's time to eat. When your body senses that it has had enough, it will send out signals to stop eating. As children, we naturally listened to these internal cues and easily followed them without question, until we were trained not to with direction from our caregivers:

"Don't eat now or you'll spoil your dinner."

"Clean your plate or you won't get dessert."

We also learned to eat with the clock instead of listening to our bodies. We eat when we aren't hungry but have told ourselves, "Oh, it's lunchtime," or we make ourselves wait until dinnertime, even though our bodies are screaming for fuel. Your body is not concerned with an external clock or set meal times. Its only concern is getting its needs met, and it communicates them to you by using physical signals. In order to hear these signals, you need to be connected with your body. Unfortunately, dieting and the development of body image issues can cause you to disconnect from your body because you're taught to see it as an object that is separate from you.

Just as you must disconnect from your body to ignore your hunger, you are also disconnecting from it when you eat past the point of full. Often times, we *do* hear our body signal us that we've eaten enough, but we choose to override that signal and eat past full for various reasons (it's there, I paid for it, I don't want to waste it, etc.). I invite you to take a really good look at the stories you are telling yourself to justify overeating, like the belief that you should clean your plate because other people are starving, for example. If this is a tape that plays in your mind, have you ever stopped to question that belief? How does your overeating offset someone else's experience of starvation? Your overeating affects only *you*. Another belief to look at (if it's one of yours) is thinking that you need to "get your money's worth" at a buffet, which leads you to piling up your plate or going back for seconds, thirds, and fourths. Are you really getting your money's worth when you overeat and cause yourself to store the extra food as fat on your body? Does it make it worth your money that your clothes don't fit and you feel terrible about yourself? I know bringing light to these truths can seem a little harsh, but if you don't stop to question the beliefs that are driving your actions, you and your body will continue to pay the price.

If you've been disconnected from your body for a while, don't worry. Your internal operating system is still running, and you can easily get back online with it with a little awareness and practice. First, you'll want to get to know the difference between physical hunger and emotional hunger. Understand that these cues are going to be different for each person. I wouldn't be able to tell you what your communication signals are because I don't live in your body. It will be your job to pay attention to yourself and take notes like a science experiment.

Physical hunger starts in your body and travels to your mind. Your body senses it needs fuel and sends a message to your brain that it is time to eat. Some possible physical sensations to look out for are a rumble or slight growl in your stomach, perhaps a hollow feeling in your abdomen, or a tiny bit of light-headedness due to a dip in blood sugar. If you get to the point of headaches, loud growling, and moodiness, you have let yourself get too hungry. This kind of hunger is called "Hangry" (hungry + angry = Hangry), and it is the hunger you've probably experienced on extreme diets that makes you irritable and want to devour anything that is not nailed down. Obviously, this physical state is to be avoided. The hunger you're looking for is more like a whisper. It tells you, "I'm ready for some fuel," but there is no sense of urgency in the presence of food. You can easily order or prepare your meal while keeping your health goals and your wellbeing in mind.

Emotional hunger starts in your mind and travels to your body. You think a thought in your mind, which causes a physical vibration in your body known as a feeling (bored, lonely, or sad, etc.). The hunger you think you feel is actually the desire to avoid feeling your feelings, and one way to quiet them is to eat. Eating to change your emotional state has nothing to do with your body's fuel requirements; it is used to check out, distract, or numb. This is the definition of emotional eating and the cause of unnecessary pounds on your frame. When you allow yourself to feel your emotions (a ninety-second sensation in your body caused by a thought you're thinking) and the food you eat is mostly to satisfy your physical hunger, your weight will naturally begin to shift.

A great way to stay mindful and eat with your body's cues is to use the Internal Stoplight Tool. My coach colleague Gaynor

Levisky inspired the idea for this tool when she mentioned using the imagery of a stoplight with her clients. She gave me her blessing to create my own version, and here it is:

I invite you to imagine a stoplight signal in your mind that corresponds with the physical sensations of hunger and fullness levels in your body:

FLASHING RED means you have eaten way past full and you feel uncomfortably stuffed and possibly lethargic. Critical self-talk often kicks in, and you berate yourself for overeating. You want to avoid this level of fullness as much as possible.

RED means a complete absence of hunger, and you feel satisfied and energized. Your body does not require fuel at this time. I invite you to make it a practice to not eat when your Internal Stoplight is on RED. Your body is now fueled and it does not require you to eat again until it sends you the signals of YELLOW, then GREEN.

YELLOW means that you feel slightly hungry, but there is no sense of urgency to eat. This is the whisper of hunger that signals you that it's time to begin preparing your meal or placing your order in a restaurant.

GREEN means that your body is physically hungry, and it is ready for some fuel. You notice a sense of calm as you eat your meal or snack and your food tastes especially delicious because you are actually hungry.

FLASHING GREEN means that you let yourself get way too hungry and you might feel a bit spacey, irritable, or feel a slight headache coming on at this point. You feel a strong urgency to eat because your brain is now demanding fuel for survival. Your ability to make healthy choices is compromised, and you could be vulnerable to overeating to compensate for not fueling your body on time. You want to avoid this level of hunger as much as possible.

This tool is super simple to use. Green light, GO. Red light, STOP. Yellow light, prepare or order your meal. You can build up thoughts in your mind that support you in using this tool: "I never eat when my Internal Stoplight is on RED" or "I always wait until my signal is GREEN before I eat something." Though it is impossibly easy once you get the hang of it, this tool requires a bit of practice in building up the body awareness of what each stoplight color represents (how physical hunger and fullness register in *your* body). Take your time and give yourself some room to make mistakes as you figure it out. You might ignore your hunger or overeat from time to time during this process, and that's okay. No big deal—just start again with the very next meal. It took repetition to disconnect from your body, and it will take repetition to get reacquainted again. It's possible to return to your natural ability to follow your internal cues, and when you set your mind to it, you will.

When you allow yourself to feel your emotions and the food you eat is mostly to satisfy your physical hunger, your weight will naturally begin to shift.

CHAPTER 37

NOURISH YOUR BODY INTUITIVELY

When it comes to choosing food to feed yourself, do you ever check in with your body and ask it what it wants? We can get so caught up in the latest food fad or get stuck in a food rut by eating the same foods day in and day out that we forget to consult our bodies' own wisdom when making decisions about the food we eat.

Your body is really smart and often wants certain foods for their specific nutrient content (protein, vitamin C, iron, calcium, etc.). Start by noticing the kinds of fuel your body is asking for and then pay attention to how well your body responds when you eat it. What's that? I can almost hear you saying, "But what if my body wants ice cream or French fries?" Well, fun food is fun and it can certainly have a place in your diet, but it does not have nutrients your body needs. Dig a little deeper to hear your body's messages and choose your fuel accordingly.

As you begin responding to your body's requests, don't be afraid to try new things or change your mind about certain food rules you've adopted. You may be surprised at first when your body asks for a kale salad for breakfast or eggs & bacon for dinner. You might discover that your body actually thrives on quality fats and that the low-fat, high-carb food pyramid guide doesn't work for you after all. Maybe your body loves it when you eat a vegan diet or it rocks on the Paleo lifestyle. Every body is different, and you are going to have to experiment with yours to find out what the right fuel is for you. You'll know which foods are right for your body because you will feel energized, you'll be able to digest them well, and they will not cause you to gain weight.

Each time your body tells you it's hungry, go ahead and ask your body what it wants. Does it want a light, cool meal? Does it want a hearty, hot meal? Is it asking for the building blocks of protein? Is it asking for the phytonutrients and enzymes found in fruits and vegetables? As you learn which fuel foods are right for your body, be sure to allow for variety as your body dictates. Let your body (not your mind) be your guide when planning your meals, when shopping in the grocery store, and when you're ordering in a restaurant. That's what intuitive eating is all about.

You know those people who say, "I eat anything I want"? Well, master the ability to nourish your body intuitively, and you will become one of those people. You will be able to eat anything you want and be healthy because what you want will be chosen from a place of true connection, peace around food, and self-love. Every time you listen to your body and choose foods that serve you instead of steal from you, it is an opportunity to change your outcome. Your choices matter, and great change can happen one meal at a time.

Every body is different, and you are going to have to experiment with yours to find out what the right fuel is for you.

CHAPTER 38

PAY ATTENTION TO HOW CERTAIN FOODS FEEL IN YOUR BODY

Your fuel is going to be different from my fuel, and how your fuel works in your body might vary with the seasons, time of day, hormonal fluctuations, and the overall state of your health. Your body is wise, and it will give you feedback on the foods you're choosing. If a certain food is causing problems, your body will alert you. If you pay attention, you can change up your fuel plan to avoid causing yourself any harm.

After you eat something, do you notice an immediate reaction when eating a particular food? Do the mucous membranes in your mouth start to tingle or itch? If so, that's an important sign to heed. Your entire digestive tract is one big mucous membrane, and if your mouth is reacting, what do you think is happening to the rest of your system as the offending food passes through and out the other end? Just saying.

Do you feel tired or listless after eating and feel like taking a nap? Food has a chemical reaction in your body when ingested. Just as some foods can amp you up (sugar or caffeine), other foods can act like a drug and bring your energy down. I watched my friend and coach colleague Deb Butler physically slump in her chair after eating some freshly baked bread for a food awareness exercise we were doing in a class. She went from her upbeat, energetic self to a lethargic lump, ready to put her head down on the table and doze off. Deb learned that her body didn't react well to the bread; needless to say, she didn't eat any more of it and easily threw the rest of the baguette in the trash.

Do you still feel hungry due to the lack of nutrients in the food you just ate? With modern farming and depleted soil, the nutrient content of our food is not what it was when our grandparents were buying groceries. Plus, there are so many lab-created non-foods lining the grocery shelves that most of what is marketed to us is completely devoid of nutrients. Your body's infinite wisdom knows when it is low on nutrients, and it will send out hunger signals in hopes that there might be something it can actually use in the next meal or snack you eat. If the majority of the food you eat lacks vitamins and minerals, your body will be disappointed in what you've provided and will keep asking for more food until it gets what it needs. You can be overfed and undernourished at the same time.

Is your digestion "off"? Do you burp up food hours later? Are you bloated and gassy? Is your elimination is too frequent or infrequent? You may or may not know this, but your gut is also known as your second brain. Your brain and your intestines are made up of the same type of cells that developed while you were gestating in the womb. That's why when you think a particularly strong thought, you feel a "gut reaction." Your brain is not going to be happy if your digestion is off, and you could experience mood swings, brain fog, and even depression. If your body is speaking to you through your digestive tract, I encourage you to take this communication very seriously. You can support your brain and heal your body by getting your digestion in good working order.

If you are looking for more information on healing and nutrition, my go-to resource is Underground Wellness.com, run by Sean Croxton. Since finding Sean's website and taking action on what I learned, my health has never been better. I was fortunate enough to stumble upon one of his YouTube videos, and I was hooked from the moment I heard him say, "Yo, what's up, y'all!" Sean has interviewed dozens and dozens of experts in the fields of health and nutrition and has compiled a wealth of information on his website. His podcasts on iTunes are my most favorite! I pick out the topics that interest me, load up my iPod, and listen to the recordings while walking, gardening, and cooking. Sean asks great questions, and from the answers the health experts offer, I make note of what speaks to me the most. I then experiment with what I learn from the podcasts and let my body tell me if it likes what I am doing or not. I discard anything that doesn't work for me and keep only the things that do. I invite you to do the same with any new ideas you decide to try out.

Are you willing to do an experiment on yourself in order to learn how to hear what your body is trying to communicate to you? If so, I invite you to track what you eat for at least a week or two. This is NOT a calorie-counting journal of diet days gone by—this is a valuable tool to help you connect with your body and hear what it is telling you. Write down what you ate and then describe in detail how you felt while eating and how you felt afterwards. Notice your energy level. Notice how you are digesting your food. Notice your mental clarity—or lack thereof. Also, write down the time you ate so that you can see how long certain foods and certain food combinations last before you begin to feel hungry again. You can use the data you collect to better care for your wonderful, amazing body and enjoy the kind of radiant health that you deserve.

Your body is wise, and it will give you
feedback on the foods you're choosing.
If you pay attention, you can change up your
fuel plan to avoid causing yourself any harm.

CHAPTER 39

WHEN COMFORT FOOD BECOMES DISCOMFORT FOOD

To desire comfort is natural and normal. As babies, we cried when we needed a diaper change; we cooed when we were cuddled; we cried out when we were hungry; and when we were fed, it felt soothing. As we grew up, we might have been given a lollipop to help us stop crying after a doctor visit, or we were given a cookie after a bad day at school, or a chocolate pudding cup if we fell off our bike and scraped our knee. With repetition, we have learned to equate food with comfort, and we have taken that belief into adulthood, resulting in us using food to comfort ourselves.

What's so interesting about this is that most of the time after an episode of comfort eating, we end up feeling worse. Do you ever overeat food you think will comfort you and then end up feeling terrible afterward? Do you ever think or say things like this to yourself after overeating?

"I feel bloated and sick."
"I feel tired, and my mind is foggy."
"I feel guilty, disappointed, and I hate myself!"

If your answer is YES, then I have to ask you, what part of this result feels comfortable to you? My guess is that you feel *uncomfortable*— both physically and emotionally after overeating food originally intended to make you feel better. If this is your experience, then I invite you to look at it another way. Instead of calling it "comfort food," tell yourself the truth by calling it what is really is—*discomfort food*.

Now, the food itself is not the problem, just the way it's being used. Perhaps this shift in your thinking will reduce or eliminate the habit of using food to comfort yourself, especially since you have acknowledged that it doesn't actually work. There are other ways you can provide comfort to yourself that do not require using food. There is also the option of exploring why you think you need comfort in the first place. Often, it's to escape an emotion you don't want to feel in the moment. Emotions are caused by the thoughts you think. By managing your mind, you will no longer need comfort and can once again savor your favorite foods as they are meant to be enjoyed.

CHAPTER 40

SEE YOUR STOMACH AS SACRED SPACE

A couple of years ago I was eating lunch in San Francisco with my friend and coach colleague Lisa Hayes. She a took bite of something on her plate and made a face: "That's not very good. There's no way I'm wasting my stomach space on that!" I loved this imagery and decided to adopt this way of thinking on the spot.

When you are eating in a connected way, you'll notice that the amount of food it takes to take you from hungry to satisfied is not a whole lot in volume. You can eat again in a few hours when your body tells you it's hungry again, but for that particular meal, the available space in your stomach is valuable real estate. Therefore, it's important to be mindful about what you're putting into your body. I was trying to explain this concept to a group of coaching students in a class I was teaching, and it dawned on me that the space in our stomachs is *sacred*. I choose to believe this, and it leads me to use that space to care for my body now.

This is what a Thought Model (from Chapter 18) would look like on this topic:

Circumstance: Stomach space
Thought: The space in my stomach is sacred, and I choose to use that space to care for my body.
Feeling: Reverence
Action: Eat with full awareness (taste, aroma, temperature, texture, quality, and amount)

Result: Connected eating that fully serves my body

Imagine a place that you consider sacred. It could be a church, synagogue, temple, or in the example I'm going to use here, a pristine redwood forest. It's peaceful, tranquil, and the ecosystem is working in perfect harmony within it. Now imagine that you decide to pollute this tranquil space by spray-painting graffiti on the trees, dumping a vat of crude oil into the crystal-clear stream, and then begin jack-hammering to destroy the peaceful silence. You would never dream of doing any of that, right? Why? Because it's Sacred Space.

Now imagine your stomach is Sacred Space. Imagine not polluting it by being super careful about introducing foods that do not destroy the ecosystem. Imagine not overfilling the sacred space within you to the point where you feel uncomfortable. Imagine filling your stomach with just enough life-giving foods that leave you feeling light, energetic, and clear-minded.

Your stomach *is* Sacred Space. Stop using it as a garbage disposal. Stop using it to avoid feeling your feelings. Instead, use the way you nourish your body as a portal to better health and a deeper connection with yourself. When you begin seeing your stomach as Sacred Space, soon enough you will begin treating it that way, and shifting what you put into it becomes an effortless act of love.

The Sacred Space of your stomach is valuable real estate. Be choosy about what you put into it.

CHAPTER 41

REMIND YOURSELF, "I DON'T DO THAT ANYMORE"

If you've been emotionally eating for a long time, the pattern can be so strong that even when you are not experiencing the negative feelings that you usually push down with food, you still might notice yourself eating when you're not hungry or picking junk food over more nourishing options simply out of habit. When I work with clients, one of the first things they practice is being aware of the habits they've been performing on autopilot. A great tool to increase your awareness of the choices you're making is keeping a journal. Writing down what you eat and how it makes you feel physically is super important data to collect so that you can really see how your choices are affecting you. When you start seeing that your energy crashes after a sugary snack, or you can hardly concentrate after eating a bagel, or your stomach starts to cramp right after eating ice cream, you begin to understand that your body is communicating to you through these signs and symptoms. Your body doesn't like what you're doing, and it's letting you know.

If you've recognized that some of your habits are hurting you or your body somehow and you've decided that you want to change, one of the best tools to practice is reminding yourself, *"I don't do that anymore."* Since your actions are driven by the way you think, when you tell yourself that you no longer do something, you are less likely to do it.

I recently checked in on a client to get an update on how she was doing after our last session. When we first started working together, she was going through the fast food drive-thru a lot and always felt physically sick afterwards. We were successful in finding out why she was overeating, but she was still having trouble stopping the drive-thru habit at first. She had already learned how thoughts drive behavior, so I gave her the thought, *"I don't hurt my body anymore"* to practice in between sessions. It dawned on me that she hadn't mentioned her drive-thru habit in the last few weeks we worked together, so I asked her about it in the follow-up email I sent. She was happy to report that she had stopped going through the drive-thru. She said that the thought, "I don't hurt my body anymore" has helped her to treat her body better overall.

I personally use this thought a lot, especially as I push my cart through the aisles at the supermarket, feeling enticed by all the goodies on the shelves. My mind tells me that I should buy a chocolate bar or two, but I know from experience that I will cause my body to have a sugar crash if I do that, so I whisper to myself, "I don't hurt my body anymore" and peacefully head towards the check-out line. I'm not denying myself the chocolate. I can certainly have it if I wanted it. It's just that these days, I want good health and a clear mind more than I want the temporary experience of eating a food that doesn't feel good in my body. This little reminder helps me stay in alignment with that.

What is a habit you know causes your body harm that you want to stop doing? I invite you to begin practicing this thought and then follow up with the action you want to do instead. You can use variations of this thought for any habit you want to change, for instance, "I don't buy stuff I don't need anymore" or "I don't let people take advantage of me anymore." What will you not be doing anymore from here going forward? I wish you all the success in making that happen.

POWER THOUGHTS
FOR SECTION SIX

Listening to my body's internal cues is a natural thing for me to do.

I'm getting really good at hearing my physical hunger and fullness signals.

When it comes to picking out the food I eat, I let my body lead.

I am open to trying new foods.

I'm willing to drop old food rules and experiment to find out what works best for *my* body.

I easily pass on foods my body does not like.

It's not comfort food if I feel physically or emotionally terrible after eating it.

I am learning to treat my stomach as Sacred Space.

My stomach is valuable real estate, and only worthy food gets in.

I want good health and a clear mind more than I want the temporary experience of eating a food that doesn't feel good in my body.

INNER WISDOM ACCESS QUESTIONS
FOR SECTION SIX

1. What are the ways I've been ignoring my body's signals? (I eat past the point of physical fullness, I push myself to stay up late when my body wants to sleep, etc.)

2. What are my specific signs of physical hunger to look out for that tell me my body requires fuel? (slight rumble or hollowness in stomach area, etc.)

3. What are my specific physical signs of fullness to look out for that tell me it's time to stop eating? (the absence of hunger, blood sugar stabilizes, etc.)

4. If I were to ask my body, what kinds of food would it choose for its next meal? (A big salad? A juicy steak? Fresh berries? Chili beans and rice?)

5. What are the reactions I have to some foods that I already know about? (I don't digest bell peppers very well, my skin breaks out after I drink milk, cheese makes me constipated, etc.)

6. What are the foods I use to comfort myself?

7. How do I feel *physically* when I eat them?

8. How do I feel *emotionally* when I eat them?

9. What would I be doing differently if I treated my stomach as Sacred Space?

10. What are the things that I know don't serve me that I don't want to do anymore?

SELF-LOVE PRACTICES
FOR WEEK SIX

• Continue making daily entries in your food journal. Add in the two awareness tools as described below.

• Choose at least one thought from the list of Power Thoughts to practice this week. Feel free to practice any others that you feel drawn to.

• Learn to let your body lead by answering the Inner Wisdom Access Questions for Section Six in your journal. This will help you go back to using the inner guidance system that already exists in your body and care for it intuitively as nature intended.

• Practice honing your hunger and fullness cues by using the Internal Stoplight Tool every time you eat or drink something. In your food journal, log what color your Internal Stoplight is on BEFORE *and* AFTER you eat/drink to increase awareness and uncover patterns in the way you're feeding your body.

Internal Stoplight Symbols:

FR (Flashing Red) = Uncomfortably full, possibly lethargic

R (Red) = Satisfied, still energetic

Y (Yellow) = A whisper of hunger, time to prepare or order your meal

G (Green) = Hungry, no sense of urgency to eat

FG (Flashing Green) = Way too hungry, strong urgency to eat, likely to overeat

Food Journal Example:

7:30 am   2 eggs, 1 piece of toast, ½ an apple, black coffee (G/R) *Feeling just right*

9:00 am   Latte (R/FR) *Was still full from breakfast, now feeling overfull*

2:15 pm   Large roast beef sandwich, side salad, iced tea (FG/FR) *Waited too long before lunch, ended up overeating*

6:30 pm   Bowl of tomato soup, 2 pieces of bread (G/R) *Feeling just right*

7:20 pm   2 scoops of ice cream (R/FR) *Was still full from dinner, feeling overfull now, one scoop probably would have been just right.*

- Practice paying attention to the effects your food and drink choices are having on your body. How does that item make you feel after you eat/drink it? (Energetic? Tired? Bloated? Jittery?) Are you able to digest it well? Since you're already keeping a food journal to practice listening to your hunger and fullness cues, you can make notes about the effects you're noticing in your body underneath the food or drink you consumed.

Practice ranking FEELING GOOD way
above looking good. When you feel good on the
inside, you can't help but shine on the outside.

SECTION SEVEN

SELF-CARE IS SELF-LOVE IN ACTION

CHAPTER 42

MAKE YOUR SELF-CARE A PRIORITY

If you were to make a list of the top five priorities in your life, where would your self-care rank? When I ask my clients to come up with a list of their priorities, many gasp when I point out that they had left themselves off their list entirely. Those who actually did list their health tended to put it somewhere near the bottom, and the very few who listed their health at the top probably wanted it to be, but their daily actions that were focused on everything *but* their health described a very different story. When asked why they think there is a lack of self-care in their daily routine, the most common reason I hear is, "I don't have time." When you say that you don't have time to take care of your body, you are essentially saying, "It's not a priority to take care of my body."

The state of your body doesn't just happen to you; you make dozens of choices each day when it comes to caring for your body. Self-care goes way beyond your body, too. It includes everything that influences your mind, like who you choose to spend your time with, what kind of TV programs you watch, what type of magazines you read, and how you speak to yourself. Your daily habits and patterns are cumulative and have a direct result. Keep doing what you're doing if you like where you are and what you have, but if you want something different, you will have to take different actions. You will also have to change who you have been in order to become who you want to be, meaning that if you're not currently a person who makes self-care a priority, you will need to become someone who does.

I invite you to look at self-care as skill building. All habits are skills we practice and master until they become automatic. Think of brushing your teeth or frying an egg for breakfast. There was a time when you didn't know how to do that and had to learn. Now you can do it without thinking very hard about it, right? If you are not already a person who takes great care of yourself and you want to be, you will likely be adding in some new self-care actions to your wellness routine. As with any skill building, the beginning of this process is almost guaranteed to be imperfect, so I invite you to stick with it, even if it feels hard or fruitless at first. By staying committed to your new practices, you not only give your body time to create results, but you also build trust with yourself by keeping your word and following through.

I'd like to take a moment and connect with all the caregivers who are reading this book right now. I am a caregiver myself, and I have lived both ends of the self-care spectrum (from non-existent to making my self-care a priority). If you're always putting someone else's care before your own, I invite you to rethink that strategy. It's imperative that you take great care of yourself *first* because if something happens to you, how will you be able to care for your ill spouse or your aging parents in your charge? For you moms out there, please believe me when I say that self-care isn't selfish, and it isn't taking away from your kids. Imagine all that you are *giving* to your kids when you show them what self-care looks like. You are their greatest teacher, and you have a wonderful opportunity to lead by example as you live the lessons you want your children to learn. If you are a caregiver of any kind, my hope is that you will see how important your self-care is to those who rely on you *and* how important it is for your own experience on this planet. You deserve to be the recipient of your own energy, and it's absolutely okay to take time out for yourself to recharge your batteries. When you make your self-care a priority, everyone benefits, especially you.

You have nowhere else to live but in the body you are in right now. When you think of it that way, doesn't it make you want to treat it better? Even if up until now you have been taking your body for granted, even if you have neglected yourself for years, any improvement in the way you care for yourself matters and makes a difference. Don't wait until you have a health crisis to make a change. You can start today with one small self-care action. Maybe you'll decide to start going to bed on time. Maybe the action you choose will be mastering the Internal Stoplight Tool from Chapter 36. Maybe your daily gift to yourself will be taking yourself for a walk around the block after dinner each night. Pick the one single self-care action you think you'd benefit from the most and focus solely on that one until you feel ready to add in another one. As your health begins to improve and you start feeling more energized, you will inspire yourself to continue building upon your self-care practices until one day you wake up and realize, "Hey, this is just what I do now," and you will smile because you feel so awesome.

Your daily habits and patterns are cumulative and have a direct result. Keep doing what you're doing if you like where you are and what you have, but if you want something different, you will have to take different actions.

CHAPTER 43

SELF-CARE AS A DAILY PRACTICE

Your self-care practice is made up of the daily habits you engage in to keep your mind, body, and spirit as healthy as possible. This includes how you feed your body, how you move it, how much rest you get, your general grooming practices, and meditation, prayer, or inner reflection.

Each person's self-care practice will be as unique as he or she is. Everyone has different preferences and what works for one person may not work for another. That's where the adventure of self-experimentation comes in! You may gather many self-care ideas from books, blogs, magazines, DVD's, health coaches, and advice from friends, but you will want to try them out on yourself to see if they work for you or not. Just because someone else swears by it doesn't necessarily mean that it will be right for you. As you find self-care practices that make you feel great, you can add them to your ongoing self-care routine.

Keeping a self-care journal is a great way to log your progress and learn a lot about yourself and your body. You can use your journal to track whatever aspect of self-care you are working on, like the improvements you're making in your nutrition, or the all benefits you notice from getting more sleep, or logging in your fitness and making notes on the physical changes you are beginning to see. One of my clients calls it her "Joy Journal" where she logs her fuel intake, her workouts, and what she did that day to create joy in her life. Another client calls it her "Proof Journal," stating how much she loves having a notebook full of evidence proving to herself how strong and capable she is. Both of these are inspired ideas!

Another great idea is creating an environment for yourself that supports the changes you want to make. Stocking your fridge and pantry with quality food your body likes, having your workout clothes, shoes, and gear ready to go, and making your bedroom a peaceful place for a good night's sleep make such a difference and help to curb any excuse-making you might be tempted to entertain. Help yourself out ahead of time and make being prepared part of your self-care plan.

Here are the Self-care Basics:

NOURISHMENT

I covered a lot about nourishing your body in Chapters 37 and 38, so I will keep this part brief. What I do want to add here is the idea of "Eating like a Grown Up." Think of it like responsible eating—not in a disciplined way, but in a caring way. It's saying to yourself, "I'm responsible for my body, and it is depending on me. I take good care of it and provide it with nutritious food so that it will thrive." When you think about the quality of your health being in your hands, doesn't that inspire you to want to make the best decisions possible when it comes to the way you eat?

Many of the nutritional decisions you make will be in the grocery store. For ease and efficiency, it helps to have a grocery list with you when you go shopping. After much trial and error, I use the notes I've made in my journal to help me make my grocery list. I keep a list of types of food and specific brands that have passed these three qualifications:

- Does it taste good?
- Does my body digest it well?
- Do I feel great when I eat this?

Preparing your list prior to going to the market can make food shopping a breeze. Fresh, wholesome food in your grocery bag means fresh, wholesome food in your belly, which means a fresh, wholesome YOU! Whatever you are bringing home in your grocery bag is what you will be building your body with, so be sure to choose your building blocks with love.

MOVEMENT

The human body is designed to move, and it benefits from activity for more than just weight loss. Regular exercise can help to relieve stress, aid in digestion, balance your hormones, improve your mood, and help you sleep better.

If you don't currently exercise, why not? Could it be you that you think of exercise in a certain way and that way doesn't sound appealing? Have you used exercise to make up for overindulging in the past and that has made you equate it with punishment? Do you look at fitness as WORK and end up avoiding it, thus avoiding all the benefits fitness provides, too? How would your relationship with fitness be different if you looked at it as PLAY? Play sounds inviting, yes? If moving your body is FUN, you are more likely to do it! Try opening up yourself to broader ideas of movement, like dance class, yoga, or paddle boarding, etc. Many cross-fit gyms and yoga/Pilates/Barre studios offer free or minimal-fee introductory classes so that you can try it out before committing to a membership. My favorite forms of movement are walking up and down the hills in my neighborhood and taking hula hoop dancing classes at my community recreation center. Both are so pleasurable that neither feels like exercise to me. This is a far cry from the non-existent relationship I used to have with exercise before I changed the way I thought about it.

I love it when things are spelled out for me and my mind goes, "Wow! That makes so much sense!" The idea helped me to make fitness a regular part of my self-care routine was this: If you exercised for one hour per day, six days a week, that would add up to 24 hours in a month. Would you be willing to spend the equivalent of one day per month on improving your health? I don't know about you, but when I look at it this way, getting my fitness in is totally doable. You don't have to commit to an hour or to 6 days a week, but I invite you to move your body in some capacity that feels good to you.

To make sure I follow through with my exercise plan, I use a technique I like to call, "Taking the Window." The Window is that block of time you know you could be using for fitness and if you don't take it when it's available, it's likely you won't get your exercise in at all that day. We've all been there and can relate, right? Think of The Window as a valuable opportunity to give yourself all of the benefits that come with exercise. I've never heard anyone say, "Gosh, I really regret working out today." Have you?

The inner workings of your body are a dance of hormones that affect the quality of your health and your outlook on life. Adding a component of fitness to your day can improve your mood and overall sense of wellbeing so greatly that you will notice a difference if you miss it. One of my clients developed a love for the benefits of exercise so much that she once said, "When I don't get to exercise, I find that I am thirsty for it." Wow, thirsty for exercise. What a cool thought to think! What kind of thoughts could you choose to think that will make you want to love your body up with some exercise? Get out your journal and pen and write them down. I also invite you to write out all of the reasons *why* you want to add fitness to your self-care routine. Remember in Chapter 13 I talked about motivating yourself with a Positive WHY? Your beliefs about why it's important to care for your body this way will be the fuel that drives your actions, and the sum of your actions will be the results you create for yourself.

SLEEP

Getting enough sleep is one of the best healing habits you could ever cultivate for yourself. You repair both your body and mind as you sleep due to the many processes happening during the hours of 10:00 pm and 6:00 am. As I've said before, our bodies still have primal coding, and we follow the 24-hour cycle of the sun (it's called the Circadian Rhythm). Your body does its best repairing between the hours of 10:00 pm and 2:00 am, and your mind does its best restoration between the hours of 2:00 am and 6:00 am. Try to make it part of your self-care practice to sleep during these hours if you can.

Our caveman ancestors often slept in total darkness, and this brought on the melatonin production necessary for sleep. When you have nightlights on in your bedroom or lights coming from your TV or computer, this can disrupt your melatonin production and affect your ability to fall asleep naturally. Either covering up these light sources in your bedroom or wearing an eye mask can make a huge difference in your quality of sleep. Unplugging would be even better, as the electronic waves can mess with your brain. If you sleep with your phone or tablet on your nightstand, be sure to turn it to airplane mode at bedtime, so that it is not transmitting a signal so close to your head as you sleep.

If sleep is an issue for you, there are other things you can experiment with, like reducing your caffeine intake or not consuming anything caffeinated in the afternoon and evening. For some people, they need to stop eating for a few hours prior to bedtime while others need to have a snack right before bed to avoid waking up hungry in the middle of the night when their blood sugar drops too low. You also might need to experiment with the timing of your exercise if you think it could be affecting your sleep in any way. Use your journal to chart your experiments as you figure out the right recipe for a good night's sleep.

One super cool thing about sleep is that twilight time in the few minutes right before you fall asleep and the few minutes just as you are waking up. Your subconscious mind is more accessible during those brief windows, and you can use it to your advantage by practicing your Power Thoughts and setting your intentions for the day. Think of it as the perfect time to update the software in your brain!

SPIRITUAL NOURISHMENT

As you build your self-care practice, be sure to nourish more than just your body. Your mind and soul need nourishment, too. Here are some ideas to get you started:

- Connecting with nature (walks, hikes, swimming in a lake or the ocean, etc.)
- Having a deep conversation with a friend
- Attending service at your place of worship
- Yoga or Meditation
- Creating or viewing art
- Writing
- Making or listening to music
- Dancing
- Spending quality time with your pets
- Reading a book
- Making love

All of these ideas and more help to raise the serotonin levels in your brain. Serotonin is the feel-good chemical that naturally lifts your mood. It is mostly manufactured in your gut out of the amino acids found in the food you eat (specifically L-Tryptophan), but you can also boost the serotonin production in your brain with the expression of *gratitude*. Recognizing what's good in your life and feeling grateful for it is very nourishing to the spirit. A spiritual practice I invite all of my clients to do is to keep a Gratitude Journal. You can have a separate one or you can use the journal you've been using all along on this *Love Yourself Lighter* journey. I recommend writing down three things you are grateful for at the end of each day. This teaches your brain to scan for good throughout your day since you know you'll be writing it down later. With practice, your brain becomes accustomed to seeking out the good in almost everything. You will automatically reduce emotional eating with this kind of mindset because the pleasant feelings you create for yourself do not need to be numbed out with food.

CREATE A SELF-CARE LIST

One of the exercises I often suggest to my coaching clients is coming up with a list of ten daily self-care practices. It can include what you're already doing to take care of yourself, plus some of the things you want to experiment with. Why ten? It works as a great awareness tool that shows you where you're at percentage-wise with your self-care routine. Say you did eight things on your list today. That means that your self-care was at 80%. Say you only managed to do four things on your list. This is not an opportunity to judge yourself, but rather it brings awareness to the fact that your self-care was only at 40% that day. You can then take a look at why and see if you can make some different choices tomorrow to bring your percentage up a little bit. Having your list in plain view is a great visual reminder to help you remember the commitment you've made to yourself. I make mine up on the computer with a nice font and print it out on pretty paper to tape up next to my bathroom mirror where I will see it every day as I brush my teeth. This is my current self-care list so you can get an idea:

1. Brush & floss my teeth, morning and night
2. Shower and dress for the day as if I might run into Oprah—or my future husband
3. Choose my fuel from as many local, organic sources as possible
4. Eat according to my body's hunger and fullness cues
5. Take vitamin and mineral supplements
6. Get outside for some fresh air and sun on my skin for the serotonin boost and vitamin D production
7. Take a walk or practice hoop dancing for fitness
8. Take off my makeup before bed
9. Reflect on my day and journal about it
10. Turn off electronics by 9:15 pm, Lights out by 10:00 pm

Your self-care list is likely to change with the seasons, and it will also change as you evolve. You can refine it as needed, but it's always a good idea to print one or handwrite it so that you can put it up where you can see it every day. Repetition is key in making your habits automatic. This means providing yourself with good care on the weekends, too. So many people abandon themselves on the weekends, saying that they'll start over on Monday. Why not use the weekends for your benefit? How can you have fun and care for yourself at the same time? Ask yourself that question, and your brilliant brain will come up with an answer for you. Each time you do something wonderful for yourself, no matter how small, be sure to give yourself credit for it. Self-acknowledgement goes a long way; it will inspire and motivate you to continue with your self-care practice on a daily basis because you *want* to, not because you have to.

CHAPTER 44

DRESS YOUR BODY WITH LOVE

Is your closet divided into two sections: Boring clothes that fit and fabulous clothes that you can't get one leg into? Do you keep telling yourself that you will treat yourself to nice clothes when you lose weight, only to watch months and possibly years go by, and you're still wearing the same kind of drab, shapeless outfits that you don't feel good in? Do you believe on some level that you don't deserve nice clothes unless you are thin? If any of this resonates, know that you are not alone. Millions of people feel uninspired by the clothes they wear or even feel depressed when getting dressed each day. If being stressed about what you are going to wear, hating the outfit you have on, or criticizing your reflection in the mirror is a familiar daily ritual for you, do not make the mistake of blaming it on your body. The relationship you have with your wardrobe happens in your mind. What you think of yourself and what you think you deserve is manifesting in your closet. You can tell a lot about what you think of yourself by the clothes you choose to buy and wear.

What is the story your current wardrobe is telling about you? Is that the story you want to convey? The clothes you wear make a statement. What statement would you like to be making?

"I like who I am."

"I matter to me."

"I take good care of myself."

Everyone has a different sense of style, and what conveys these messages for one person may look very different on someone else. The main thing is that you want your wardrobe to convey *to yourself*, "I love and care about me." You can achieve this by making the act of dressing your body well part of your daily self-care routine.

Despite what you may have been believing, you deserve to wear nice clothes now, today, instead of sometime in the future that is contingent on your size. Clothing does not have to be expensive to be stylish, and what is stylish and pleasing can only be defined by you, not by what fashion trends are dictating from season to season. If you are fashion-challenged like I was, I recommend gathering inspiration from the many great fashion resources available to you; use books, TV shows, YouTube tutorials, blogs, and Pinterest.com style boards to help you pick out clothing that is flattering to your specific body shape. Choose fabrics in colors that look good on you and textures that feel good against your skin. When you seek to delight your senses of sight and touch, clothing can turn out to be a bonus source of pleasure.

As you select garments to try on, forget about assigning any meaning to the size tags in clothing and pick out clothes that fit your body. Think of size tags only as a guideline since sizes can vary greatly from brand to brand. Practice speaking to yourself kindly when trying on clothing items in the dressing room so that you can leave feeling as peaceful as when you went in. Remind yourself that every garment is cut and sewn differently depending on the particular designer's imagination, so if something doesn't work, never blame your body. Your body is not wrong. The garment is simply not right for your body, so keep trying on other things until you find something that is. Trying on several things or stepping outside of your fashion comfort zone might take a bit more effort when you go shopping, but it will be worth it to have clothes you like available to wear right there in your closet.

Speaking of closets, one of the kindest things you can do for yourself is to overhaul your closet and dresser and get rid of anything that does not fit, that does not look good on you, or that you do not like wearing. Clothes that don't fit not only take up space, but they can also be an energetic drain on your psyche when you look at them as reminders of what you can't wear. Other energetic drains are stained clothes, ratty underwear, clothes with holes or missing buttons, and shoes that are scuffed or need re-heeling. Repair what you can and donate or dump the rest—especially that ratty underwear! Yes, that may mean that you will have very few items left once the purge is over, but there is something very empowering about opening up your closet and knowing that every single thing in there not only fits but looks great on you. This makes getting dressed each day a pleasure instead of a minefield of mental torture.

As you build back your wardrobe, be very picky about what you bring in. If you don't feel like a million bucks in it, then don't spend your hard-earned bucks on it. You are forming a new relationship with clothes now, one where you are using the act of getting dressed each day as an opportunity to show yourself how important you are to yourself. Most people don't think of using their clothing as an expression of self-love, but it is. Creating a wardrobe that feels like love is the kind of self-care that will ripple out like a pebble in a pond; when you feel great about yourself, you can't help but contribute your gifts to the world.

When you create a wardrobe that feels like love, there is something very empowering about opening up your closet and knowing that every single thing in there not only fits but looks great on you.

CHAPTER 45

ELIMINATE UNNECESSARY STRESS TRIGGERS

When you hear people talk about the stress in their lives, they speak of it as if it is something happening *to* them. Rarely does anyone take responsibility for the stress they feel—probably because they have no idea that they are the ones causing it with their own thinking. Nothing outside of us can cause us to feel stressed, but we can orchestrate our lives in a way that supports us in thinking thoughts that serve us better.

Here are some are some ways we trigger our own stress and their remedies:

MEDIA "NOISE"

Have you noticed how much negativity we are exposed to on a daily basis?

- News shows that sensationalize murder, war, and financial doom & gloom
- Talk shows with couples fighting over paternity, cheating, and exposing life-altering lies
- Print ads that simulate violence towards women or unattainable standards of beauty that shame them into buying products

- Gossip magazines and websites that tear down celebrities, especially for their looks
- Reality shows that depict heinous behavior and never-ending catty remarks made behind each others' backs or straight to their faces

When you are bathed in this much negativity on a regular basis, can you see why it's so easy to engage in mean self-talk and self-destructive behavior? When you are surrounded by examples of hate, it's only a matter of time before you turn that inward on yourself.

Remedy: There is an old saying, "You become like the company you keep." While this usually applies to the people you surround yourself with, extend that a little further and include other things that keep you company—like heavy news shows, violent movies and television, back-stabbing reality TV programs, and magazines that teach you to criticize yourself and others. Experiment with limiting your exposure these sources of negativity or eliminate them altogether. Instead, seek out content that offers examples of the kind of behavior you want to emulate. Fill your mind with images of nature's beauty, good news, and anything else that brings you closer to who you want to be.

CLUTTER

If unmanaged, clutter can accumulate in your environment, and every day that you face piles of stuff in your home, stacks of paper on your office desk, or bags of gear or forgotten debris filling up your car, overwhelming thoughts can add to an already chaotic mind. The stress you feel might also be compounded as you search for your keys or that important document you needed, like yesterday. You may even cause yourself to worry constantly about what people might think of you if they saw how you're choosing to live.

Remedy: Clearing up the clutter in your life is a self-care action. When your environment is free of clutter, you give yourself the space to live more fully because your mind will be free to focus on other things. The task of clearing clutter can seem insurmountable at first, but if you break it down to one small section at a time, you build confidence with each success. Start with a junk drawer and move your way up to releasing any pockets of clutter that weigh you down. A way to keep clutter to a minimum is to nurture the relationship you have with yourself. The more connected you are with yourself, the less you need stuff to fill the void. Eventually, when you have cultivated a deep connection within, there is no longer a void to fill.

SELF-CREATED DRAMA AND CHRONIC COMPLAINING

How much drama do you experience on a daily or weekly basis? Are you generating a lot of emotional pain for yourself with the stories you are weaving in your mind? Are you inserting yourself into other people's business and making yourself upset over things you have no control over? Many people will subconsciously seek out drama as a distraction from paying attention to their own lives. Worry is the main tool most will use to create drama for themselves. My friend Lisa Hayes calls worrying "meditating on sh*t." Abraham-Hicks calls it "praying for what you don't want." Whatever drama you engage in, your body releases stress chemicals that can take a toll on your health and wellbeing over time.

Another distraction from yourself and your life is chronic complaining. When you complain, you strengthen the neural connections of those negative thoughts in your brain. You are also causing yourself unpleasant feelings as you tell the story over and over again to anyone who will listen. Each time you complain, you're left sitting there with the unpleasant feelings you just created for yourself. How are you going manage them? Up until now, you may have been using overeating to shut those feelings down. If you are someone who beats herself up for overeating and then ends up feeling worse, you might be setting yourself up for even more overeating to shut down *those* feelings, and this cycle becomes a whole new drama of its own.

Remedy: Whenever drama knocks on your door and invites you to engage, did you know that you have the option of declining the invitation? When you notice yourself entertaining lots of negative or worrisome thoughts, practice declining the drama and switch your mind's focus to an entirely different topic. Or if your thoughts are particularly stubborn, allow them to surface but keep reminding yourself, "These are just words in my mind. They have no power unless I decide to give them some."

When you notice yourself getting worked up about what's going on in other people's lives, you might want to step back and ask yourself, "If I'm so busy in *their* lives, who is living *my* life right now?" Spending time in other people's business leaves less time for your own. Reel that energy in and spend it on the kind of self-care practices that strengthen you and make your life so much richer. When you're happy with your own life, you automatically lose interest in the drama going on in other people's lives.

As far as complaining goes, complaining is the language of Victim Mentality. It drains your energy and causes you to be blind to all that's already wonderful in your life. When you're complaining, you are making a choice to focus on the negative instead of focusing on the positive. This is not a great strategy since you get more of what you focus on (if you complain a lot, you will attract more things to complain about). The obvious remedy is to stop the habit of finding fault in everything. You can do this by scanning your world for all that's good in it. Make it a game to seek out the best in every person and situation. There will always be things that have the potential to delight you if you choose to look for it.

JUDGING OTHERS AND GOSSIPING

Sometimes we judge and gossip about other people in an attempt to make us feel better about ourselves, but do we really feel better for it? When we judge others, it is a sure sign that we are judging ourselves just as harshly (if not more), and that never feels good.

The funny thing about judging other people is that it never has anything to do with the other person—it always has to do with you 100% of the time. Your judgment comes from the way you think. The person sitting next to you could absolutely adore the person you just made a snarky comment about, so your comment speaks of *your* character, not theirs. Another interesting fact about judging others is a coaching term called, "If you spot it, you got it," meaning that whatever you are judging about the other person, you also have the same trait in yourself. You may not express it in the exact same way, but if you look for it, you will find it. For example, say you judge someone for lying in a Facebook post, but meanwhile you falsify your timecard every time you're late for work—you are lying, too, just not in the same way. Because you are dishonest, it stands out to you when you think other people are being dishonest. Oh, and by the way, just because you are projecting your thoughts onto someone else doesn't make it true. Unless you have facts, your opinion is just that—an opinion. Even if you do have facts, your judgment *still* speaks of you because that is how you are choosing to look at it. Everyone you meet teaches you something about yourself if you're open to the lesson. The more they annoy you, the more you need to pay attention.

Remedy: Instead of judging and gossiping, love is another option you could choose. When you catch yourself judging others or gossiping about them, stop and acknowledge you're doing it, then purposely choose to project love their way instead. Look for at least one trait they possess that you admire and say it out loud. The "If you spot it, you got it" rule works both ways—when you recognize a positive trait in another person, it's because you also have it, too! Building other people up in this way can help you raise your opinion of yourself. Every time you say something nice about someone, you are essentially saying something nice about yourself.

To identify your unnecessary stressors, I invite you to get out your journal and pen and start jotting down the places in your life where you are participating in the options outlined above. Be as real with yourself as you can here. The more truthful you are, the more energy you will have at your disposal once you've dropped the draining habits. When you decide to direct your energy back towards yourself in a positive way, you can't help but feel more connected to yourself and your life. You may notice that you begin to feel happier, kinder, and more patient. Your thinking becomes more calm and clear with practice. Your intuition may become sharper because you are no longer distracted by all the noise around you and within your own mind. Though you may never be 100% stress-free, it is possible to live an extraordinary life when you choose to live it in the drama-free zone.

CHAPTER 46

BUILD A SUPPORTIVE TRIBE

You may never have considered the idea that your friendships have anything to do with your self-care practice, but since the people you surround yourself with can greatly influence the way you think and the choices you make, this is an important aspect of your life I invite you to take a look at.

When you think of the members of the Circle of Influence you've chosen for yourself, what do you do when you spend time together?

Do you engage in self-bashing talk with your friends about how fat your thighs are and how many rolls you can count on your stomach?

Are you competitive? Do you and your friends engage in a silent competition of who can eat the least at lunch or who has the biggest house/ring/cabin by the lake?

Is the time you spend together filled with whining and complaining about all the things in life you think are unfair?

Energy leaks come in all forms, including friendships and relationships. How do you know it's an energy leak? You feel drained in their company, you feel drained even after you part, and sometimes you feel like you need a shower to wash the negativity off of you. In all fairness, you are engaging in the relationship and contributing to it somehow—otherwise the friendship wouldn't exist. As you begin evolving, however, expect that some of your friendships might change.

The reason why you connect with someone is because you are a vibrational match on some level. You are drawn to different people for different reasons, but in order for a friendship to develop, you have to have something in common. As you grow on this journey and become more of the person you want to be, your energy will begin vibrating at a higher frequency. Many of your friends will support you and adapt to the changes you make. Some may even join you on the journey, but there also may be others who resist change and who want to continue staying small in their lives—and would prefer it if you did, too. The friends who don't grow with you will stay at the frequency they were at when you met, and it will not match with the frequency you are expanding into as you begin to live more authentically. Sometimes that means that the friendship needs to be altered and perhaps you don't spend as much time together or you shift the topics away from the negativity you once shared as a common bond. Sometimes it means allowing the friendship to end. When friendships end, it doesn't necessarily mean that it's a bad thing—it simply means that the friendship is now complete. You can still have love for the person, even if he or she is no longer in your life.

Because we have primal wiring for connection, women especially fall into the trap of wanting to be liked. We worry about what other people think of us, and too often we value the opinion of others higher than we do our own. We betray ourselves in many ways, like saying yes to things when really we mean no or trying to be something we're not, all because we are afraid of how we will look to other people if we followed what's truly in our hearts. The good news is that it doesn't have to be this way. All that needs to change is the way you think. Let me share with you the beliefs I've adopted that have helped me to drop the people-pleasing syndrome and attract stellar friendships that enrich my life in so many ways.

1. **Not everyone is going to like you and that's okay.** Your worth and value do not hinge on getting everyone's approval, so don't waste your time on the haters. That's not the energy you want in your sphere anyway. A much more important question to ask than "Do they like me?" is "Do I like *them*?" Who do you enjoy hanging out with? Who do you want in your Circle of Influence? You get to pick your friends, so pick people you genuinely like who genuinely like you back.

2. **You teach people how to treat you.** What you accept is what you will get. Ignoring passive-aggressive comments or flakiness could backfire on you because those who do it might think that it's okay with you if you don't speak up. Communicate what you will not tolerate and encourage behavior you like. If someone still doesn't treat you well, you don't have to take it. You deserve quality friendships, and any person who doesn't treat you right does not deserve space in your life.

3. **If your heart is not in it, it's okay to say NO.** Only say yes to a request or an invitation if it's something you truly want to do—otherwise you will be grousing or seething inside the whole time. If a person gets upset with you for saying no, that's his or her prerogative. If your saying no changes the friendship in any way, then that's a friendship you might want to re-evaluate. You should never have to do anything to be someone's friend.

4. **Don't change so people will like you.** If you aren't being yourself in a friendship or relationship, then people don't like *you*—they like the lie you are presenting to them—and it's exhausting to keep that lie going. Just relax and be yourself and the right people will love the real you.

5. **Let people be who they are.** We all have our quirks, and nothing is more taxing on a friendship than the stress of having to follow someone else's idea of who you should be or how you should act. When you let people be who they are and love them anyway, they will feel free to be themselves in your presence, and this is a beautiful space for real intimacy and true connection to thrive. ** This does not mean tolerating bad behavior—see #2.

The more you value yourself and treat yourself well, the more you will instinctively seek out friends who are like-minded and on a similar path. Their presence in your life nourishes your spirit, and you feel energized in their company and long after you part. Petty competitiveness doesn't exist, but rather you inspire and encourage each other to go for your dreams, and you celebrate every triumph and success made along the way. Speaking the truth is a great tool for separating your people from those who are not your people. When you are real with everyone you meet and show up as yourself, your people will be able to recognize you. Those who don't vibe with you will naturally fall away to find their own tribe. Surrounding yourself with a supportive tribe is one of the best gifts you could ever give yourself because life is so much sweeter when you share it with those who truly see you and lovingly remind you of how amazing you are when you forget sometimes.

Your worth and value do not hinge on getting everyone's approval, so don't waste your time on the haters. That's not the energy you want in your sphere anyway. Create friendships with people you genuinely like who genuinely like you back.

POWER THOUGHTS
FOR SECTION SEVEN

I thrive when I am the recipient of my own energy.

I make it easy to care for myself by always being prepared.

Exercise is just another way I show myself how much I matter to me.

Nourishing my spirit is as important as nourishing my body.

I am learning to speak kindly to myself when trying on clothes.

I choose to wear clothes that say, "I like who I am."

I am responsible for any stress I cause myself when I think stressful thoughts.

When I catch myself judging others, I choose to send love their way instead.

I'm open to relationships changing as I evolve and grow.

My Circle of Influence is filled with people who inspire me to be the best version of myself.

Inner Wisdom Access Questions
For Section Seven

---

1. The reasons why I want to make my self-care a top priority in my life are…

2. What is the one self-care action I know would benefit from the most if I were to focus on it? What is the most effective strategy I can come up with to make this happen?

3. How can I make my environment more supportive to maximize my self-care efforts?

4. What's my current relationship with exercise? What would I like it to be? What are the thoughts I would need to think to make exercise a regular part of my self-care routine?

5. What are my favorite ways to nourish my spirit?

6. How would I like to feel when I get dressed every day? How can I dress my current body so that I can feel that way now?

7. From the information outlined in Chapter 45, what are my specific stress triggers? Am I aware of any others that are not listed? What are they?

8. Which stress trigger would I like to change first and why? (Remember, having a Positive WHY will support the actions you decide to take when making a change.)

9. Who is in my current Circle of Influence? How do I feel in each friendship and why? Is there anything that I would like to change in these friendships and how will I do that?

10. How do *I* want to show up as a member in another person's Circle of Influence?

SELF-LOVE PRACTICES
FOR WEEK SEVEN

- Continue using the Internal Stoplight Tool as you make your daily entries in your food journal. Also, continue to pay attention to how certain foods feel in your body. If a particular food does not agree with your body (indigestion, sugar crash, etc.), consider skipping it and choose other foods that make you feel great instead.

- Choose at least one thought from the list of Power Thoughts to practice this week. You're probably getting pretty good at this by now, so pick a couple more to practice if you want to. The more good thoughts that fill your mind, the better!

- Prepare your mind as a foundation for your Self-care Practice by answering the Inner Wisdom Access Questions for Section Seven.

- Create a list of ten self-care actions you think you would benefit from if you did them on a daily basis. This can include things you are already doing for self-care (like brushing your teeth), plus the things that might require more thought and effort (like planning your meals or paying attention to your hunger and fullness cues). Hand write or print out this list and put it up where you can see it every day as a reminder of the way you want to care for yourself. At the end of each day, count up the things on the list that you accomplished and see where you are percentage-wise in your self-care for that day. Give yourself credit for the things you did and then brainstorm some thoughts in your journal that will motivate or inspire you to apply some more energy to the other things on the list you may have skipped. Make it fun by playing a game with yourself to see how many days in a row you can go where you keep your self-care at 70% or above.

And the day came when the risk to
remain tight in a bud was more painful
than the risk it took to blossom.

~ Anaïs Nin

SECTION EIGHT

LIVE LIKE YOU
LOVE YOURSELF

CHAPTER 47

LOVE YOUR LIFE NOW, NOT LATER

"Getting ready to live." Wow. How many of us have spent way too much time in this place, waiting until we are thin before we really start living our lives? The truth is that we are already living our lives right now in the bodies we currently have. It's just that the life we are settling for pales in comparison to the more vibrant version waiting for us in the wings. So many of us deny ourselves the things we could be enjoying now because of the thoughts we have about our bodies or because of the belief we have that we need to wait on a perfect set of circumstances to materialize before we can be fully and completely happy. When you stop to think about how precious life is, isn't it absurd that we put our lives on hold *on purpose*?

When I think about the preciousness of life, my mind goes straight into my memory banks and transports me to an Alaskan cruise ship and a woman named Margaret. I had seen Margaret all week on this particular vacation. How could I miss her? Every day she was dressed in sequins, loud colors, and feather boas, even during the daytime. I guessed Margaret was in her late forties or early fifties and while she was usually surrounded by friends, I began to notice that every night without fail, she'd be dancing away in the disco, shaking her booty in a gown fit for the Miss America pageant, always the last one on the dance floor after all her friends had turned in for the night. I thought to myself, "Wow! This woman sure is loving life!"

Turns out she was loving life—loving it to the fullest because she didn't have much of it left. See, I learned towards the end of the cruise that Margaret was dying. This cruise was her last big hurrah, and she had invited all of her best friends to join her. *That's* why she wore sequins and feather boas during the day. *That's* why she danced until dawn. She wanted to experience all of the possible joy to be had before her body gave up on her. Margaret showed me by example that no matter your circumstances, you are completely in charge of your experience. I could tell by her actions that her mind was set on the thought, "Have as much fun as you can!"

What is *your* mind set on? Like everyone else on the planet, you have a belief about how much of life's goodness you think you deserve. That belief acts like an internal thermostat in your mind and depending on where you have it set, it will determine how much goodness you allow yourself to have. Some people have their Goodness Gauge set on high and seem to experience boundless joy and abundance while others have it set so low that the joy in their lives is almost non-existent. What is your Goodness Gauge set at? If it is set lower than you'd like it to be, you can change the setting by changing how you see yourself. When you begin to think more highly of yourself (as discussed in Chapter 24), you naturally align yourself to attract more goodness into your life. Like attracts like, remember?

For those of you who subconsciously resist receiving more, this might be a slower process, and you can begin to inch your Goodness Gauge up higher by *consciously* engaging in your desired experiences and getting used to the feelings of having more until it begins to feel natural. Just as it takes practice to get to the place where you automatically take better care of your body, it will take some practice to automatically allow yourself to receive abundant goodness when you've been used to experiencing less. The more you do the things on your Desired Experience List, the more you will evolve into your Best Self. It's not the doing of the activities themselves but who you become in the process of acting like you deserve those things now. Sometimes you have to fake it until you make it. When you override your limiting thoughts and take action anyway, you are telling yourself that you *do* deserve good things, and your choice to give it to yourself provides proof for your new belief.

I invite you to compile a list of all of your desired experiences. No matter how silly or unrealistic you think it may be, if the thought of it lights you up, it goes on your list. What are the things you've been wanting to do but have been putting off?

Do you want to...

- Learn a foreign language?
- Go back to school and take a specific course or finally get your degree?
- Create beautiful art with paint, clay, watercolor, photography, or other media?
- Learn how to do the Tango, or the Rhumba, or the West Coast Swing?
- Take a cooking class and expand your culinary repertoire?
- Swim in crystal blue waters, take a stroll through a lush forest,

or hike to the tallest peak and take in the gorgeous views?

- Write a book? A screenplay? Your memoir?
- Build a chicken coop and enjoy fresh eggs from the chickens you raise?
- Learn how to drive a stick shift?
- Buy yourself that pair of diamond earrings you've always wanted, or that stunning handbag you've had your eye on, or perhaps a new car?
- Experience romantic love in a mutually satisfying relationship?
- Travel to the corners of the earth you long to see with your own eyes?
- Visit people you haven't seen in a long time and tell them how much you love them?

After writing out your list in your journal, I hope you are not even thinking the thought, "It's too late for me to _____." It is *never* too late. My own mother, having never earned her Master's Degree due to raising her children as a single mom, went back to school at age sixty-nine and earned her Master's Degree in Gerontology at age seventy-one. Exactly one month after graduation, she was hired by a local non-profit and continued to work as a social worker for senior citizens for the next ten years. She loved her job and never felt happier. By following her dream, she not only got to feel a sense of personal satisfaction, but over one hundred seniors benefited from all that she gave as a Service Coordinator at their place of residence. She recently retired at the age of eight-one.

Whatever your dreams or desires are, they are worth pursuing. Say you're fifty years old and you plan on living until you are at least ninety-five—that means you could potentially have forty-five years left! That is a lot of freaking time! You can make it great or you can make it suck. But you won't make it suck—not after reading this book. You are going to love yourself enough to do the all the things that speak to your heart, and your life will be beautiful because you've decided to make it that way.

CHAPTER 48

HAPPINESS IS A HABIT

Why do we want the things we want in life? Ultimately, we want the feelings we think we will feel once we have/do/or achieve the things on our Desired Experience List. We might want to feel proud, accomplished, excited, successful, or loved, but for most of us these feelings boil down to feeling *happy*. People often make the mistake of believing that happiness is a destination somewhere out in the future that can only be reached by taking some kind of action. The state of happiness is not a place you arrive at but a feeling you choose to feel over and over again each day. Happiness does not come from a thing, an experience, or another person, but from the thoughts you're thinking in your mind *about* that thing, experience, or person. Nothing outside of you can make you happy because nothing *outside* of you can cause feelings *inside* of your body—only you can do that. This means that waiting on a future circumstance like weight loss is fruitless because you can create happy feelings for yourself right now with the thoughts you choose to think.

I invite you to think of a happy memory. It could be picturing your child's smile, or the moment you were given some really great news, or something quirky your beloved pet does that cracks you up. You could also think of something that's *about to happen*, like the vacation you are packing for or anticipating the party you are throwing for someone you love. For me, it's recalling any time my friends and I were laughing uncontrollably about who knows what.

Thinking about it right now causes me to feel a warm sensation radiating in my chest, and my lips are curling into a smile on my face. What are you feeling in your body as you think your happy thought? Can you see that you are causing yourself to feel happy in this moment and it's not caused by the circumstance itself (since it's either already passed or it hasn't happened yet)? The happiness you feel is happening in your mind, and you are in complete control of it.

I do want to take a moment and bust that myth about happiness that you're supposed to be in some kind of euphoric state all of the time. This is an unrealistic expectation. The happiness you feel will ebb and flow with the thoughts you're thinking and what you choose to focus on. Even the happiest people on the planet will have negative thoughts that surface as often as every day, but perhaps they choose not to fixate on them or have trained their minds to seek out the positive in their world instead. Your focus cannot be in two places at once, so when negative thoughts pop up in your mind (and they will), you can either entertain them or you can choose to direct your thinking elsewhere. Expressing gratitude is a tool I use a lot to help me shift my mind. Being thankful for the cup of tea in my hand, or for the awesome friends I have, or for my dog napping next to me as I work, draws my focus to the abundance of goodness I already have. Not only does this shift my mind away from negative thinking, but this also moves my Goodness Gauge up higher. When you express gratitude for all that's good in your life, you open yourself up to receiving more.

When I think of all the things in life we can be happy about, it makes me wonder why any of us ever set our sights so low as to hang our happiness on how much we weigh. We no longer have to think so small. We can increase our ability to feel happy by practicing happiness each day. Choose to see the best in people. Notice the beauty in your surroundings. Seek the company of people who inspire you or make you laugh. Choose to see the best in yourself. Look for what is already awesome about you and celebrate it. When you practice feeling happy, a happy person you will be.

People often make the mistake of believing that happiness is a destination somewhere out in the future that can only be reached by taking some kind of action. The state of happiness is not a place you arrive at but a feeling you choose to feel over and over again each day.

CHAPTER 49

USE YOUR LIFE TO INSPIRE OTHERS

A few years ago, I had the great pleasure of being on the support crew at a weight loss seminar held in Scottsdale, Arizona. I was surrounded by like-minded women the entire time, and I made an effort to connect with as many of them as I could. When the lunch break rolled around, I was invited to scrunch into a cozy booth with a group of seminar participants. As we chatted, some of the women expressed their fears about sharing good news with their friends. One woman said that she didn't post on Facebook that she got a 4.0 for fear that her classmates would get upset. Another said that she didn't tell her co-workers about attending the seminar, fearing they might judge her for how she spent her time and money. Being the coach that I am, I asked both of them, "What if the sharing of your achievements or the way you treat yourself well actually *inspired* other people?" By the looks on their faces, I could tell that this thought never crossed their minds.

Was I surprised by this? No. In our culture, Mean Girl behavior is alive and well. Many of us have been conditioned to avoid shining too brightly for fear of being judged by others. This is such a shame because the reality is, for every hater who is quick to judge, there are many more people in this world who are desperate to live a fuller life and would absolutely go for it if they knew that it was possible. To my lunch companions, I offered the idea that sharing their good news with others might actually help another person to blossom and that hiding their joys and successes might potentially rob someone of the inspiration she needed to elevate to the next level.

Funny enough, it turned out that we had proof of this right there at the table. One of the women had previously attended a powerful coaching retreat and shared that information with her friend. That friend became inspired and shared the information with another friend, and now the three of them were sitting at the table together at this empowering seminar. Had the first woman been too afraid to share her story, she would have missed the opportunity of inspiring her peers to connect with themselves and better their lives.

When you stop playing down what's great about you and let yourself shine, you inspire other people to give themselves permission to do the same. This is very healing because we waste a lot of energy trying to suppress our inner light with heavy things like the weight struggle. Sometimes people need to see how it's done in order to take action, so when you love yourself and treat yourself well and you express it in the way you live your life, you are providing an example of what's possible for them. Go ahead and live your life out loud because you never know who you are inspiring by doing so.

When you stop playing down what's great about you and let yourself shine, you inspire other people to give themselves permission to do the same.

CHAPTER 50

YOU ARE MEANT FOR GREAT THINGS

Nobody wants to hear this, but there is a reason why you manifested a weight struggle in your life. The extra weight you've been carrying represents the disconnection you have from yourself, and when you address the emotional component of the weight struggle, you provide yourself with an opportunity to heal what needs to be healed. Nothing has gone wrong where your weight is concerned. Your path was always meant to go this way. You are not broken. You are not damaged or defective. You never were. You are whole. You are empowered. You are capable. And you are wise. Believe it my dear, because it's true. It always has been. You just haven't able to see it because faulty thinking has been blocking your view. Hopefully, as you navigate your way through this *Love Yourself Lighter* journey and you are taking the steps to rewire old thinking, you will begin telling yourself a new story that is closer to the truth of what an amazing person you already are.

As you reinvent yourself into a person who no longer measures your worth by your weight, what are you going to do with all of that energy you used to spend spinning in the weight struggle? This is a serious question. Imagine that size, weight, food, or calories were no longer topics of interest to you anymore: What would you be doing with your life that's different from the way you live it now?

We all have a purpose on this planet. You may be called to invent something, or create beautiful art, or raise thoughtful children, or teach important work. Whatever your unique purpose is, your body is your vehicle for you to do your work in the world. Think of your self-care habits (fitness, good nutrition, adequate rest, and play) as ways to align your vessel so that you can best give the world the gifts that only you can give.

Something wonderful is out there calling your name. Can you hear it? It's time to drop the negative mind chatter and open your heart to the call. You are meant for great things. What is the legacy you want to leave behind? And what are you going to do to make sure that happens? What is the one big risk you're resisting? That is probably the one your soul wants you to take next. Whether your reach is global, local, or just within your own family or circle of friends, your contribution matters, and it is important to those you are meant to influence.

Of course, the most important person you will ever influence is yourself. You have a wealth of wisdom within to draw upon and you've already been tapping into it by answering the Inner Wisdom Access Questions at the end of each section. You can also mentor yourself by connecting with your Future Self in your mind and asking her how she succeeded at something. Think of the You in the future who has already achieved the goal you have set for yourself. Your goal can be anything—a fitness goal, a business goal, a financial goal, an art or writing project—you name it! In your journal, have your Future Self write out the steps she took to achieve the goal, including all of the thoughts she used to stay motivated and inspired to complete it. You will now have a blueprint of the steps to follow, and when you take them, you will meet up with your Future Self who is already there! The best way to succeed at anything is to believe that it is already done.

The adventure of your life is before you, and you are now armed with new tools to help you create whatever you want for yourself. You have learned how to change the way you think, and you have learned how to treat yourself like you are someone you love. Though life will still throw some challenges your way from time to time, know that you will be better able to handle it with the Wellbeing Mind you've cultivated for yourself by using the tools in this book. You are one of a kind, Dear Reader, and my wish for you is that you fully enjoy who you are and you relish the life you design for yourself from here forward. Many years from now, may you leave this planet with a heart overflowing with beautiful memories, instead of a pocketful of dreams unlived. Choose to live each day like you love yourself, and you can begin collecting those memories now.

POWER THOUGHTS
FOR SECTION EIGHT

I'm open to moving my Goodness Gauge up to a higher setting.

It's never too late to do something I want to do.

I make my life as beautiful as I want it to be.

I don't chase happiness; I choose it for myself every day.

When I express gratitude for all that's good in my life, I open myself up to receiving more.

When I shine, I inspire others to do the same.

I no longer measure my worth by my weight.

The answers I seek are already within me.

I am meant for great things.

I deserve to live a life I love.

INNER WISDOM ACCESS QUESTIONS
FOR SECTION EIGHT

---

1. What is my Goodness Gauge set on? High? Low? Somewhere in-between? Why is it at this setting?

2. What's my plan for raising my Goodness Gauge higher?

3. From my Desired Experiences List, what is the first thing I want to do? Why do I want to do this?

4. What are the things I already have that I am grateful for?

5. What have I been inspired to do after seeing someone else do it first?

6. How can I use my life to inspire other people?

7. How has my weight struggle been perfect for my journey thus far?

8. What is the new story I want to tell about myself?

9. From the depths of my soul, I know my purpose is to…

10. What thoughts do I need to think in order to show up and live my purpose/offer my gifts to the world?

SELF-LOVE PRACTICES
FOR WEEK EIGHT

- Continue using the Internal Stoplight Tool as you make your daily entries in your food journal. The more you practice this tool, the more automatic it becomes.

- Choose at least one thought from the list of Power Thoughts to practice this week. There are so many good ones to choose from, so practice the ones you like the best. These are the kinds of thoughts you want driving the outcomes in your life!

- Open yourself up to living a fuller, richer life by answering the Inner Wisdom Access Questions for Section Eight.

- Have your Future Self write you a letter of encouragement to support you in following your dreams and living a life you love. Write it on beautiful stationery and mail it to yourself. Reading your own words will be very motivating and inspiring because you will know that you already have the power within to succeed.

An Invitation

Dear Reader,

I hope you have enjoyed reading *Love Yourself Lighter*, and I hope that you have come away with several tools and ideas that will help you create the peace you seek with food, your weight, and your relationship with yourself and your body.

Though this book has been written as a self-coaching program, if you think that you would greatly benefit from a more hands-on approach, I invite you to reach out to me for private coaching. It would be an honor to be your personal guide through the chapters, and help you uncover the Why behind your weight, teach you how to reprogram your thought-patterns, and help you achieve the goals you set for yourself.

To schedule a complimentary 30 minute Discovery Session, please go to my website, www.SuyinNichols.com, and click on the "Let's Connect" page. Fill out the boxes and submit your request. I will personally answer your coaching inquiry, and I will be happy to discuss your coaching needs with you. I look forward to working with you!

My very best always,

Suyin

Made in the USA
Charleston, SC
11 April 2015